INTRODUCTION TO BOOKKEEPING

Award in Bookkeeping

Qualifications and ..ework

AAT Level 1 Aw ..ookkeeping

British Library Cataloguing-in-Publication Data

A catalogue record for this book is available from the British Library.

Published by
Kaplan Publishing UK
Unit 2, The Business Centre
Molly Millars Lane
Wokingham
Berkshire
RG41 2QZ

ISBN 978 1 78415 640 4

Printed and bound in Great Britain.

Kaplan Publishing would like to thank Deborah Seed and Julie Hodgskin for their contributions towards the production of this publication.

CONTENTS

If you are studying the Level 1 Certificate in Accounting, please note that the other assessed units are covered in depth in a dedicated Study Text for this qualification, including the Award in Computerised Accounting (ISBN 978 1 78415 639 8).

Kaplan Publishing also produce a Study Text for the Level 1 Award in Accounting (AAT Access) should you choose to study for this qualification in addition to the Level 1 Award in Bookkeeping (ISBN 978 1 78415 641 1).

INTRODUCTION

HOW TO USE THESE MATERIALS

These Kaplan Publishing learning materials have been carefully designed to make your learning experience as easy as possible and to give you the best chance of success in your AAT assessments.

They contain a number of features to help you in the study process.

The sections on the Unit Guide, the Assessment and Study Skills should be read before you commence your studies.

They are designed to familiarise you with the nature and content of the assessment and to give you tips on how best to approach your studies.

ICONS

The study chapters include the following icons throughout.

They are designed to assist you in your studies by identifying key definitions and the points at which you can test yourself on the knowledge gained.

 Definition

These sections explain important areas of Knowledge which must be understood and reproduced in an assessment

 Example

The illustrative examples can be used to help develop an understanding of topics before attempting the activity exercises

 Activity

These are exercises which give the opportunity to assess your understanding of all the assessment areas.

UNIT GUIDE

Level 1 Award in Bookkeeping

Overview

The Level 1 Award in Bookkeeping consists of four units:

- Introduction to bookkeeping
- Working within bookkeeping
- Bookkeeping and accounts
- Spreadsheet software

The first three of these units are assessed via a computer based test entitled Bookkeeping and accounts. Spreadsheet software is assessed via a computer based project.

Learning Outcomes and Assessment Criteria - Level 1 Award in Bookkeeping

Bookkeeping and accounts (BKAC) enables students to understand the role of a bookkeeper and accounting terminology and to be able to process transactions through the accounting system and produce a simple trial balance.

This two hour assessment consists of 13 tasks in one section. Students will normally be assessed by computer-based assessment and will be required to respond to CBT tasks in a variety of ways, for example using multiple choice, true/false, drag and drop, pick lists, text select, linking boxes, gap fill tools and AAT purpose built question types to reflect real workplace activities.

The assessment criteria for the three individual units are as follows:

Introduction to bookkeeping

The aim of this unit is to enable students' understanding of the basic role of bookkeeping within different types of organisations, and to know and understand the basic terminology used in bookkeeping.

1.   Understand the job role and career path for a bookkeeper

1.1   Outline the job role of a bookkeeper

1.2   Outline how the role of the bookkeeper fits within the business organisation

1.3   Outline how bookkeeping can become a career pathway

2.   Understand different types of business organisations

2.1   Give examples of different types of business organisation

2.2 Define the organisations known as:
- sole trader
- partnership

3. Know the terminology used in bookkeeping

3.1 Identify the difference between a bookkeeper and an accountant

3.2 Explain the correct use of two of the following (minimum) bookkeeping terms:

petty cash imprest system; sales; purchase; customer; supplier; receipt; payment; income; expenditure

3.3 State how two (minimum) of the following bookkeeping documents are used: petty cash voucher; purchase order; invoice; credit note; statement of account

Working within bookkeeping

The aim of this unit is to provide the student with knowledge of the general principles of single entry bookkeeping, VAT, cash and credit transactions, different systems and processing information, and in general the roles and responsibilities of individuals working in bookkeeping.

1. Understand single-entry bookkeeping

1.1 Explain single entry bookkeeping

1.2 Outline the books used in single entry bookkeeping

2. Know the general principles of VAT

2.1 State when a business must register for VAT

2.2 State the various rates of VAT in general use:
- reduced rate
- standard rate
- exempt
- zero rate

3. Understand what is meant by both cash and credit transactions

3.1 Explain what is meant by cash sales

3.2 Explain what is meant by cash purchase

3.3 Explain what is meant by trading on credit

3.4 Identify the various documents needed to record a credit sale or purchase

4. Understand the principles of coding and batch control

4.1 Explain why a coding system is used for financial transactions

4.2 Outline the use of batch control

5. Understand how to process information in the books of prime entry (excluding the Journal)

5.1 State where to find financial information for entry into the bookkeeping system

5.2 State where to enter relevant information in the books of prime entry (excluding the journal)

5.3 Outline the need to cross check totals for accuracy

6. Understand responsibilities when working in a bookkeeping environment

6.1 Outline the responsibilities relating to security of data when dealing with customers, suppliers and other external agencies

6.2 Identify where to gain authorisation for expenditure and when dealing with queries related to various financial transactions

Bookkeeping and accounts

The aim of this unit is to test the student's ability to undertake basic bookkeeping practices and to process source documents that underpin accurate record keeping.

1. Know how to complete financial documents.

1.1 State the purpose and identify the content of financial documents

1.2 Calculate sales tax, trade discount, settlement (cash) discount, price, price extension on invoices and credit notes

1.3 Complete financial documents

1.4 Check the accuracy of financial documents

2. Be able to record cash and credit transactions in books of original entry.

2.1 Enter invoices and credit notes into the appropriate day books

2.2 Transfer the total(s) of the day book(s) to the respective ledger account(s)

2.3 Post individual transactions from the day books to personal ledger accounts

2.4 Record cash book transactions and credit transactions using double-entry bookkeeping

3. Be able to prepare bank reconciliation.

3.1 Update a cash book (bank balance) using details from a bank statement

3.2 Recalculate the closing bank balance

3.3 Prepare a bank reconciliation statement using appropriate information

4. Be able to understand the petty cash imprest system.

4.1 Enter the opening balance in the petty cash book

4.2 Analyse petty cash vouchers to appropriate analysis columns

4.3 Balance and cross tally the petty cash book totals and analysis columns

4.4 Transfer totals to ledger accounts as appropriate

4.5 Restore the imprest

5. Be able to extract a trial balance from ledger accounts.

5.1 Balance ledger accounts

5.2 Bring down account balances to the following accounting period

5.3 Extract the trial balance from the ledger and cash book

Learning Outcomes and Assessment Criteria – Level 1 Spreadsheet Software unit

Spreadsheet software

The aim of this unit is to enable students to understand the uses of a spreadsheet and populate a spreadsheet with a variety of different data. It also focuses on the use of formulas to provide information in a variety of formats, knowing how to use various approaches to present spreadsheet information accurately and effectively.

The time allowed for the computer based project assessment is 1 hour and 45 minutes. Learners should be able to construct a spreadsheet containing a minimum of five columns and seven rows of data and text, including headings. As most organisations now use spreadsheets, the skills tested will give learners the ability to use functions to produce professional-looking and meaningful spreadsheets.

1. Use a spreadsheet to enter, edit and organise numerical and other data

1.1 Identify what numerical and other information is needed and how the spreadsheet should be structured to meet needs

1.2   Enter and edit numerical and other data accurately

1.3 Store and retrieve spreadsheet files effectively, in line with local guidelines and conventions where available

2. Use appropriate formulas and tools to summarise and display spreadsheet information

2.1 Identify how to summarise and display the required information

2.2 Use functions and formulas to meet calculation requirements

2.3 Use spreadsheet tools and techniques to summarise and display information

3. Select and use appropriate tools and techniques to present spreadsheet information effectively

3.1 Select and use appropriate tools and techniques to format spreadsheet cells, rows and columns

3.2 Identify which chart or graph type to use to display information

3.3 Select and use appropriate tools and techniques to generate, develop and format charts and graphs

3.4 Select and use appropriate page layout to present and print spreadsheet information

3.5 Check information meets needs, using spreadsheet tools and making corrections as necessary

Summary

Achievement at Level 1 reflects the ability to use relevant knowledge, skills and procedures to complete routine tasks. It includes responsibility for completing tasks and procedures subject to direction or guidance.

Knowledge and understanding

- Use knowledge of facts, procedures and ideas to complete well-defined, routine tasks.
- Be aware of information relevant to the area of study or work.

Application and action

- Complete well-defined routine tasks.
- Use relevant skills and procedures.
- Select and use relevant information.
- Identify whether actions have been effective.

Autonomy and accountability

Take responsibility for completing tasks and procedures subject to direction or guidance as needed.

STUDY SKILLS

Preparing to study

Devise a study plan

Determine which times of the week you will study.

Split these times into sessions of at least one hour for study of new material. Any shorter periods could be used for revision or practice.

Put the times you plan to study onto a study plan for the weeks from now until the assessment and set yourself targets for each period of study – in your sessions make sure you cover the whole course, activities and the associated questions with answers at the back of the Study Text.

When working through your course, compare your progress with your plan and, if necessary, re-plan your work (perhaps including extra sessions) or, if you are ahead, do some extra revision/practice questions.

Effective studying

Active reading

You are not expected to learn the text by rote, rather, you must understand what you are reading and be able to use it to pass the assessment and develop good practice.

A good technique is to use SQ3Rs – Survey, Question, Read, Recall, Review:

1   **Survey the chapter**

    Look at the headings and read the introduction, knowledge, skills and content, so as to get an overview of what the chapter deals with.

2   **Question**

    Whilst undertaking the survey ask yourself the questions you hope the chapter will answer for you.

3   **Read**

    Read through the chapter thoroughly working through the activities and, at the end, making sure that you can meet the learning objectives shown within the summary.

4   **Recall**

    At the end of each chapter, try to recall the main ideas of the section/chapter without referring to the text. This is best done after short break of a couple of minutes after the reading stage.

5   **Review**

    Check that your recall notes are correct.

You may also find it helpful to re-read the chapter to try and see the topic(s) it deals with as a whole.

Note taking

Taking notes is a useful way of learning, but do not simply copy out the text. The notes must:

- be in your own words
- be concise
- cover the key points
- be well organised
- be modified as you study further chapters in this text or in related ones.

Trying to summarise a chapter without referring to the text can be a useful way of determining which areas you know and which you don't.

Three ways of taking notes

1 **Summarise the key points of a chapter**

2 **Make linear notes**

A list of headings, subdivided with sub-headings listing the key points.

If you use linear notes, you can use different colours to highlight key points and keep topic areas together.

Use plenty of space to make your notes easy to use.

3 **Try a diagrammatic form**

The most common of which is a mind map.

To make a mind map, put the main heading in the centre of the paper and put a circle around it.

Draw lines radiating from this to the main sub-headings which again have circles around them.

Continue the process from the sub-headings to sub-sub-headings.

Highlighting and underlining

You may find it useful to underline or highlight key points in your study text – but do be selective.

You may also wish to make notes in the margins.

Further reading

In addition to this text, you should also read the 'Student section' of the 'Accounting Technician' magazine every month to keep abreast of any guidance from the examiners.

Working within bookkeeping

1

Introduction

The accounting department perform a vital role in all organisations, providing financial information to internal and external customers. In this chapter you will learn about the types of organisations in which accounting professionals work and how they provide support to other departments. In particular we will focus on the role of the bookkeeper within this process.

As information provided by accounting professionals may be commercially sensitive, it is important to understand how to handle this confidentially.

Finally, we will look at career development opportunities for bookkeepers and their professional and ethical responsibilities.

KNOWLEDGE
Introduction to Bookkeeping
1 Understand the job role and career path for a bookkeeper
2 Understand different types of business organisation
3.1 Identify the difference between a bookkeeper and an accountant
Working within Bookkeeping
6.1 Understand the responsibilities relating to security of data when dealing with customers, suppliers and external agencies

1 Business organisations

1.1 Business sectors

Before looking at the role of bookkeepers, we will first consider the types of organisation in which they work. There are three main sectors in which business organisations operate. Each of these sectors has a different purpose.

Private sector   The main purpose of business organisations in the private sector is to **make a profit** for their owners. Private sector organisations include sole traders, partnerships and limited companies.

Public sector   The purpose of public sector organisations is to **provide essential services** such as education and health care. They are funded by monies raised through taxation.

Examples include councils, NHS, Police, Fire and Ambulance services.

Charities   Charitable organisations are set up to raise money and awareness **to promote a cause or to provide services** for specific groups.

Examples of these are Save the Children and Guide dogs for the Blind. You can probably name others.

 Activity 1

Write down the names of as many charities you can think of.

Then, write down what you think each charity does for the public or for the 'common good' of society.

Then check their websites to see if what they do is what you think they do.

1.2　Ownership in the private sector

There are three different types of ownership of **private sector** organisations. The main purpose of each of these organisations is to make a profit.

Type of Business	Ownership
Sole Trader	A sole trader business is owned by one person. If the business makes a profit the owner will keep all the profits. However, if the business gets into financial difficulty, the sole trader is responsible for all the debts. A sole trader may work on their own or have several employees. The owner is in direct control of all elements and is legally accountable for the finances of the business. Sole traders may use a trade name or business name other than their own legal name.
Partnership	A partnership is similar to a sole trader business but is owned by between two and twenty people. Each partner will take a share of the profits of the business or be liable for the losses of the business.
Limited companies	When a limited company is set up it is given its own legal identity. The ownership of these companies is divided into shares of the business. Any profit made by the business is allocated to shareholders in the form of dividends, based on how many shares they hold. Shareholders have limited liability which means that they are not liable for the business's debts. If the business gets into financial difficulty, shareholders will only lose the money they originally invested. The shares of private limited companies (Ltd) are usually given to the directors of the organisation or other private individuals. The shares of public limited companies (plc) are sold on the stock exchange which means that anyone from the general public can buy them.

Activity 2

Identify the purpose of each sector by matching the sector in the first column with the purpose in the second column.

Sector	Purpose
Private Sector	To provide essential services
Public Sector	To promote a cause
Charity	To make a profit

Activity 3

Identify which sector the following organisations belong to:

	Private Sector	Public Sector	Charity
An animal welfare organisation			
Local government			
A sole trader			
A limited company			
A primary school			
An environmental conservation organisation			

2 Customers of the accounting function

2.1 The function of the accounts department

The function of the accounts department of an organisation is to provide financial information to its customers. These customers can be from inside the organisation (internal) or outside the organisation (external).

All customers will expect the accounts department to provide information which is accurate and complete, and is delivered on time.

2.2 Information for internal and external customers

Examples of the types of information that internal and external customers need from the accounts department are listed below.

Internal customers:

Sales Department	may need to know the amount of credit and cash sales for a particular period.
Marketing Department	may need to know how much money is available for advertising.
Purchasing Department	may need to know if and/or when a supplier's invoices have been paid.

External customers:

Suppliers (Creditors)	may need to know when an invoice will be paid for goods or services supplied.
Customers (Debtors)	may need to know how much they owe the business for goods and services sold.
HMRC (Her Majesty's Revenue and Customs)	may want to check the amount of invoices received and supplied to ensure the correct amount of VAT has been collected.

Definition

Function – an activity carried out in an organisation. For example, the accounting function is carried out by the staff in the accounts department.

 Activity 4

Why is it important for employees in the accounting function to treat internal customers with the same courtesy and respect as external customers?

3 Accounting function support to the organisation

3.1 Support from the accounting function

The accounting function provides help and support to all other functions within the organisation.

The managers of these other functions will rely on the information provided by accounting staff in order to run their departments effectively and contribute to the overall smooth running of the organisation.

It is very important that any information provided by the accounts department to the rest of the organisation is timely (up to date), accurate (free from errors) and complete (nothing is missing).

 Definitions

Working effectively – Completing tasks accurately and on time.

Working efficiently – Completing work as quickly as possible to required standards without making mistakes

3.2 Information from the accounting function

The table below gives examples of the key information provided by the accounts department to other functions in the organisation.

Information	Function
Management will need information about the profit or loss of the organisation. For example, they may want to know whether a particular product is making a profit or a loss, or which department is making the most profit.	Management
The manager of the production department may want to know if the department has spent more or less than budgeted. They may need to know the cost of raw materials, discounts, the cost of any machinery and the budget for any replacements.	Production
The sales function may want to know about the income received from a particular product or the level of sales each sales person has been responsible for.	Sales
Human Resources may want the total salary cost of the staff, if there is a recruitment budget and whether there are any bonuses, overtime or commission due.	Human Resources

Activity 5

The Premises manager has approached you for some help. He has some costs, present and future, that need to be met, and he is unsure of which budgets to use. He has sent you a memo, part of which is below. Fill in the gaps with the correct budget name.

I need to know how much money is left in the _____ budget to plan future repairs to the buildings.

I want to send two members of staff on a course to develop their skills so I need to apply to the _____ budget.

A couple of fire extinguishers need servicing by outside contractors. I will put the cost through the _____ budget.

Pick list

Premises	Distribution	Advertising
Training	Production	Health and Safety

4 Confidentiality

4.1 Confidentiality

Most of the information supplied by the accounting function will be financial information that may be both sensitive and/or private. Whether the information is held on paper or held electronically on a computer, accounting staff must make sure that confidential information is kept in a safe and secure way, so that it is only made available to the people authorised to see it.

4.2 Commercial information

Information held by the accounts department may be commercially sensitive. For example, the price paid for a particular product, or discounts given to customers. If a competitor of the business knew this information they might be able to use it as a competitive advantage.

4.3 Personal information

Personal information held about individuals, such as employees and customers, is protected by law. The Data Protection Act sets out rules about how personal data can be used.   The Information Commissioner's Office (ICO) is the UK's independent body set up to uphold information rights. You can find out how your personal information is protected by visiting their website: https://www.ico.org.uk

Whether personal and sensitive information is held on computer or in a paper based filing system it must be kept safe and secure. This means it must be kept away from any unauthorised access. It would be wrong to leave personal data open to be viewed by just anyone.

4.4 Security of confidential information

If you have been given sensitive information to work with it is your responsibility to keep it safe and secure. Below are some examples of how you can keep confidential information secure so that it cannot be accessed by unauthorised people. Security of information can be either physical or electronic.

Physical: Locked cabinets, cupboards, doors, and the shredding of documents all ensure that physical access is restricted.

Electronic: Electronic access by authorised personnel only can be set up by passwords and encryptions.

Example

Situation	Paper based filing system	Information held on a computer
Confidential information you are currently working with.	Any confidential information you are responsible for should be kept close by you at all times so that you are aware if anyone tries to read it. To avoid the information being seen by anyone passing by your desk, all confidential paperwork should be kept face down or in a folder until you need to work with it.	You may need to change the position of your computer screen to make sure that unauthorised people cannot see information on your computer screen as you are working. If this is not possible, you may need to move desks or offices to ensure that you can carry out the work. Sensitive information held on computers should be protected by multi-level passwords so that employees only see what is relevant to them. Never share your password with unauthorised people.
If you have to leave your workstation	If you have to leave your desk always put any confidential papers in a locked drawer or filing cabinet.	You should use the screen lock on your computer so that confidential information cannot be read by people passing your desk when you are away.
Storage of confidential information	Sensitive information should be kept in a locked filing cabinet, until it is needed.	Regular back-ups of computer data should be taken and stored in fireproof cabinets.
Out of date information	When confidential information is no longer needed it should be shredded before being recycled.	Data should be removed or deleted from computers by authorised staff from the Information Technology (IT) department.

Definition

Authorised person – Someone who has been given permission to do something on somebody else's behalf. For example, an employee who has been authorised to input confidential information onto a computer.

Activity 6

Commercial information is information that can be sold to anyone, so it does not have to be kept confidential. True or False?

 Activity 7

Below is a list of security measures.
Tick the column that you think the security measure belongs in. Some may be both types.

Security measure	Physical	Electronic
Cabinets are locked at all times and the keys held by the office manager		
All employee personal information no longer required is shredded		
Passwords are changed every thirty days		
Access to different areas of the accounting software is restricted according to employee's duties		
Access to the department is restricted by inputting the correct code into a keypad		
ID cards must be worn at all times		

5 The role of the bookkeeper

5.1 Why do we need bookkeepers?

No matter where you live or work in the world, an organisation will always need a bookkeeper.

The main reasons bookkeepers will always be needed are:

- So that the owner/manager knows the income and expenditure of the business.
- So that the owner/manager can make decisions that will improve/expand the business.
- So that the organisation pays the correct amount of taxes due.

All governments need money to finance their activities, and they get that money from businesses and individuals in the form of taxes.

5.2 The role of the bookkeeper

The role of the bookkeeper is to keep an accurate record of all financial transactions carried out by an organisation. In most organisations, each transaction is first recorded in a daybook and then transferred to ledgers using the double entry booking system. Bookkeepers are responsible for keeping these records up to date and accurate.

In larger organisations, the bookkeeping work is often separated into different business activities carried out by clerks. For example, a sales ledger clerk will produce customer invoices and statements and chase up outstanding debts. A purchases ledger clerk will keep a record of all invoices received from suppliers and process payments. Cashiers are responsible for recording all monies received and paid by the business. In smaller organisations, a bookkeeper will perform all of these activities.

Once the data has been entered, the information will be analysed by an accountant who will produce financial reports for the managers of the business. It is essential, therefore, that the information provided by bookkeepers or accounts clerks is accurate and up to date.

Bookkeepers and accounts clerks are entry level job roles, but there are a lot of opportunities for career progression by work experience and gaining bookkeeping and accounting qualifications.

5.3 Career progression – the role of an accountant

An accountant's role is to interpret and analyse the information provided by the bookkeeper or accounts clerk so that the owner/manager can make business decisions. Accountants help this decision-making process by interpreting and offering alternative strategies.

5.4 Continuing Professional Development (CPD)

When considering their professional development, bookkeepers will need to assess and look to develop their skills. Some of their career skills are professional, whereas some are their personal attributes. Professional skills include:

Professionalism	Accounting professionals should be able to demonstrate a high level of competence in their work and be able to meet the required standards of the profession.
Integrity	Accounting professionals should adopt an approach to work guided by strong moral principles. They are expected to be straightforward, honest and trustworthy.
Numeracy	Accounting professionals are expected to have good numeracy skills. They should be able to process numerical information quickly and accurately and be able to understand and explain calculations.

Literacy	Accounting professionals need to be skilled at dealing with written content.
Communication Skills	Accounting professionals need to be able to speak and deal with a wide range of people using a range of communication skills: e.g. writing, speaking, presenting, and listening.

As well as the key skills mentioned above, accounting professionals are expected to display certain personal attributes. These include:

Reliability	Employers and your team workers will need to rely on you to do the work that you promised to do.
Punctuality	Being punctual means being on time, both in terms of arriving at your place of work on time and completing a required task at an agreed time.
Willingness to learn	Showing a willingness to learn demonstrates that you are interested in your job role and the organisation. It also suggests you are not afraid of learning new skills which will help you and the organisation to develop.
Organisation	Employers will expect you to be able to complete work within an agreed time frame. If you are well-organised you are more likely to be able to complete your work effectively and efficiently.

New skills and knowledge can be acquired in a variety of ways.

Accounting professionals will undertake **formal training** to learn technical skills, for example by enrolling on a college course to take AAT qualifications. Knowledge and experience can also be acquired through **informal training** such as self-study or on the job training. Examples of informal training are given below.

Example

Job Rotation	Job rotation involves switching employees round through a range of jobs. Job rotation can mean that employees are given a wider knowledge of the organisation. It can also help the organisation if cover is needed for absent staff.
Job Shadowing	Job shadowing means working with an experienced employee who can pass on the skills and knowledge required to perform the task
Professional Journals	Professional journals are magazines written by professionals in a particular field of interest. For example, the AAT Accounting Technician magazine.
Internet/ newspapers	These sources provide up to date financial news and information relevant to accounting professionals.

The AAT's Continuing Professional Development (CPD) policy follows a four-stage cycle: Assess, Plan, Action, Evaluate. The AAT recommend that the cycle is followed at least twice each year in order for its members to develop their skills and further their career.

When considering their personal development, the AAT CPD cycle can help bookkeepers and their line managers to evaluate your performance and set appropriate development goals and targets. It also will enable them to continually assess their learning needs to keep up to date with professional developments.

Assess learning and development needs and goals.

What skills do I need to be able to perform my duties effectively?

Plan appropriate activities to meet learning and development needs and goals.

Research how skills can be developed and discuss training opportunities with your manager. It might be by enrolling on a college course, or having informal training from a colleague.

Evaluate whether the activities did meet the developmental goals.

Can I now perform the tasks the organisation needs me to?

Action the plan

Enrol on a college course/ schedule training with a mentor.

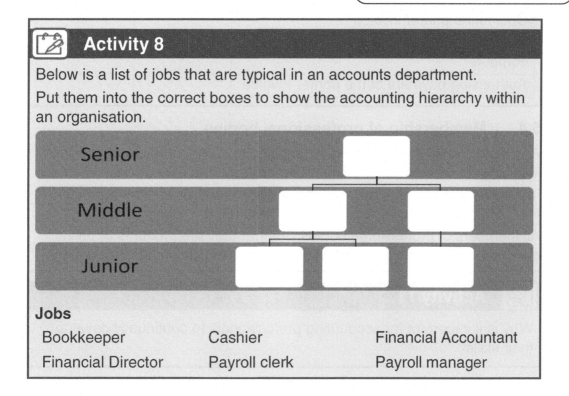

Activity 8

Below is a list of jobs that are typical in an accounts department.

Put them into the correct boxes to show the accounting hierarchy within an organisation.

Senior		
Middle		
Junior		

Jobs

Bookkeeper	Cashier	Financial Accountant
Financial Director	Payroll clerk	Payroll manager

Activity 9

Fill in the gaps from the pick list below to complete the paragraph about bookkeepers.

The bookkeeper is responsible for _____ the financial _____ of an organisation. An accountant is responsible for _____ the financial _____ of an organisation.

The _____ suggests alternative strategies, based on the interpretation of the financial information. The _____ will make the decisions.

A bookkeeper may start as a _____, but, with hard work and study, can progress to _____ accountant

Pick list

Accountant	bookkeeper	information	interpreting
manager	senior	inputting	transactions

Activity 10

Below is a list of duties that are performed in the accounting department. Tick the column to suggest who would typically perform each task.

Role	Bookkeeper	Accountant
Authorising the purchase of a new printer		
Coding the printer invoice		
Entering the printer invoice into the computer		
Authorising payment of the printer invoice		

5.4   Membership of professional bodies

A professional is someone who is qualified to carry out a task with a high level of expertise and skill. Accounting professionals are people who have qualifications in accountancy. They usually belong to a professional body such as the AAT.

All members of professional bodies whether they are students or fully qualified accountants are expected to behave ethically and professionally.

Activity 11

Why is it important for accounting professionals to continually develop their skills?

5.5 Ethical behaviour

Behaving ethically means doing the right thing at the right time. Accounting professionals are trusted by their employers to handle confidential and sensitive information in an appropriate manner.

The AAT has published a set of ethical guidelines for accounting professionals to follow, see http://www.aatethics.org.uk/code/. The following fundamental ethical principles form part of these guidelines.

- **Confidentiality** – as described earlier in this chapter, it is important that information is not disclosed to third parties, used for personal gain or shared unless there is a legal or professional duty to do so.

- **Objectivity** – accountants should remain independent and show sound judgement rather than allowing bias, personal interests or pressure from others to influence them.

- **Integrity** - this means being straightforward and honest when you perform your duties.

- **Professional behaviour and competence** – this means that you are able to perform your job to an acceptable level and provide a good service. All accounting professionals should undergo regular training to keep their technical knowledge up-to-date so that they can complete work to agreed standards, without mistakes.

Activity 12

In each of the following situations decide whether this is an example of ethical behaviour or not. For each, state which ethical principle is being considered.	Is this ethical behaviour?		Which ethical principle is being considered?
	Yes	No	
Discussing the issues one of your clients is facing when with your friends over dinner.			
Providing advice on an area of tax accounting you are not familiar with to a customer.			
Completing the accounts on time and bearing in mind all recent changes in legislation.			
Changing the contents of a report because your manager offered you a financial bonus to do so.			

6 Environmental and social responsibility

6.1 Environmental issues in business

Businesses as well as individuals need to think about how they can change the way they work in order to protect the environment for the future. An organisation's customers may consider whether businesses behave in an environmentally, ethically and socially responsible way before they will do business with them.

Many businesses have developed environmental and socially responsible policies and initiatives that benefit the internal and external customers of the business, as well as the wider society.

For example, the Unilever Group, a multinational organisation in the food and beverage industry manufactures some of the world's leading tea brands. One of the sustainability initiatives developed by the company is to work directly with the tea plantation farmers to make sure that they have safe working conditions and learn how to farm in sustainable ways, for example, by reducing the use of chemicals. Unilever also donates trees for planting and helps the local communities by building roads and schools.

http://www.unileverfoodsolutionsarabia.com/sustainability/case-studies/tea

 Definition

Sustainability means meeting the needs of the present generation without compromising the ability of future generations to meet their own needs.

6.2 Environmentally-friendly policies

All companies, large or small, can introduce policies to encourage staff to reduce the negative environmental impact of an organisation.

Examples of these sort of policies are found on the next page.

Example

Paper saving	Think before you print! A lot of paper is wasted by printing out single line emails or unnecessary copies of documents
Recycling	Central recycling points in the building for paper, food and drink cans and plastic bottles rather than individual waste paper bins.
	This could remove to temptation for people to easily throw away rubbish.
Energy saving	Ensuring that lights and computers are switched off at the end of the day.
Fuel efficiency	Installing video or phone conferencing facilities to cut down on staff travel.

 Definition

Policy – A written document explaining how an organisation does something and the procedures it follows.

Activity 13

Consider your own workplace and suggest ways in which it could become more environmentally and socially responsible.

7 Summary and further questions

This chapter looked at the different types of organisations in which accounting professionals can work. In each case, employees working in the accounting function will need to deal effectively and efficiently with internal and external customers.

Much of the information that is held in the accounting department is private and sensitive and should be treated confidentially by making sure that it is kept securely.

Finally, you learnt why it is important for accounting professionals and the organisations in which they work to behave in an ethical and socially responsible manner.

Activity 14

Complete the sentences below using the pick list provided.

_____ sector organisations are normally concerned with the provision of basic government services.

_____ are private businesses owned by one person.

_____ sector organisations are primarily concerned with making profit from the sale of goods or services. Where these businesses have shareholders they are known as _____.

Pick list

Private	Public	Charity
Sole traders	Partnerships	Limited companies

Activity 15

Match the following definitions with the correct business function.

Business function	Definition
PRODUCTION	This department sells the company's goods and services to customers.
SALES	This department is responsible for typing, collecting and distributing mail, keeping & filing records, organising meetings and maintaining resources
ADMINISTRATION	This department deals with the recruitment of new staff, the training of new and existing staff, pay negotiations and regular staff appraisals
ACCOUNTING	This department is responsible for producing the goods or services that a business provides by making best use of the various inputs.
HUMAN RESOURCES	This department is responsible for keeping records and accounts, for giving advice on budgets to other departments, and for paying wages and salaries

Activity 16

You have been working on a confidential document on your computer and have to leave the office for ten minutes to deal with a customer. How can you keep the information on your screen confidential?

Tick the most appropriate answer.

Switch the computer off	
Use the screen lock facility to lock the computer screen	
Stay at your desk	
Put some papers over the screen to hide the information from passers by	

 Activity 17

Which of the following are principles that a professional accountant should follow in order to demonstrate ethical behaviour?

Tick ALL that apply.

Confidentiality	
Flexibility	
Integrity	
Confidence	
Numeracy	

 Activity 18

Which TWO of these options is an example of a socially and environmentally responsible organisation?

Offering free lunches for staff	
Training staff to use the recycling facilities	
Keeping the computers switched on at all times	
Using video conferencing instead of travelling to customers' premises	

Answers to chapter activities

 Activity 1

Examples of charities and their goals include:

British Red Cross – to 'mobilise the power of humanity so that individuals and communities have the capacity to prepare for, deal with and recover from crisis'

Make-A-Wish – to 'grant the wishes of children with life-threatening medical conditions to enrich the human experience with hope, strength and joy'.

Oxfam – to 'create lasting solutions to poverty, hunger and social injustice'.

 Activity 2

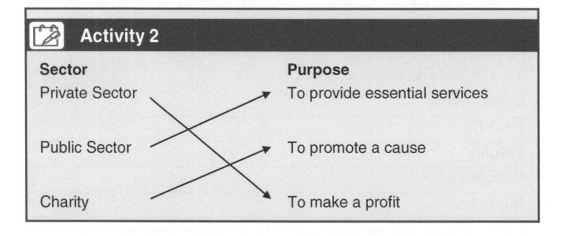

Sector	Purpose
Private Sector	To provide essential services
Public Sector	To promote a cause
Charity	To make a profit

 Activity 3

	Private Sector	Public Sector	Charity
An animal welfare organisation			✔
Local government		✔	
A sole trader	✔		
A limited company	✔		
A primary school		✔	
An environmental conservation organisation			✔

KAPLAN PUBLISHING

Activity 4

The accounting function provides support and an essential service to the rest of the organisation. If they do not provide a good customer service to other departments it can put a strain on internal relationships and result in the organisation not giving a good overall level of service to all its customers.

 Activity 5

I need to know how much money is left in the **Premises** budget to plan future repairs to the buildings.

I want to send two members of staff on a course to develop their skills so I need to apply to the **Training** budget.

A couple of fire extinguishers need servicing by outside contractors. I will put the cost through the **Health and Safety** budget.

 Activity 6

The statement is false. Commercial information is sensitive information about an organisation which could give competitors an advantage if it was disclosed. For example, if a competitor knew about the discounts an organisation offered to customers, the competitor could offer better prices to win business.

 Activity 7

Security measure	Physical	Electronic
Cabinets are locked at all times and the keys held by the office manager	✓	
All employee personal information no longer required is shredded	✓	
Passwords are changed every thirty days		✓
Access to different areas of the accounting software is restricted according to employee's duties		✓
Access to the department is restricted by inputting the correct code into a keypad	✓	✓
ID cards must be worn at all times	✓	

Activity 8

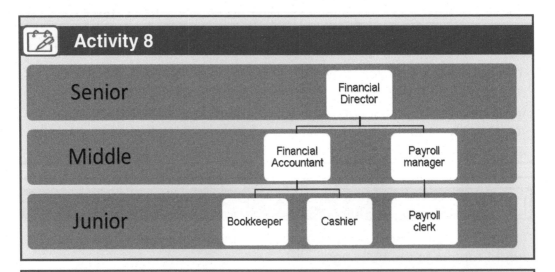

Activity 9

The bookkeeper is responsible for <u>inputting</u> the financial <u>transactions</u> of an organisation. An accountant is responsible for <u>interpreting</u> the financial <u>information</u> of an organisation.

The <u>Accountant</u> suggests alternative strategies, based on the interpretation of the financial information. The <u>manager</u> will make the decisions.

A bookkeeper may start as a <u>bookkeeper</u>, but, with hard work and study, can progress to <u>senior</u> accountant

Activity 10

Role	Bookkeeper	Accountant
Authorising the purchase of a new printer		✔
Coding the printer invoice	✔	
Entering the printer invoice into the computer	✔	
Authorising payment of the printer invoice		✔

Activity 11

Accounting professionals need to ensure that they remain competent for the work they do. They will need to keep up to date with changing regulations that affect their work. They will also need to keep up to date with technologies that help them do their work efficiently and effectively.

KAPLAN PUBLISHING

Activity 12

	Ethical?		Ethical principle
	Yes	No	
Discussing the issues one of your clients is facing when with your friends over dinner.		✓	Confidentiality
Providing advice on an area of tax accounting you are not familiar with to a customer.		✓	Integrity
Completing the accounts on time and bearing in mind all recent changes in legislation.	✓		Professional behaviour & competence
Changing the contents of a report because your manager offered you a financial bonus to do so.		✓	Objectivity

 Activity 13

There is no written answer for this activity.

Activity 14

Public sector organisations are normally concerned with the provision of basic government services.

Sole traders are private business owned by one person.

Private sector organisations are primarily concerned with making profit from the sale of goods or services. Where these businesses have shareholders they are known as **limited companies.**

Activity 15

Business function	Definition
PRODUCTION	This department is responsible for producing the goods or services that a business provides by making best use of the various inputs.
SALES	This department sells the company's goods and services to customers.
ADMINISTRATION	This department is responsible for typing, collecting and distributing mail, keeping & filing records, organising meetings and maintaining resources.

ACCOUNTING	This department is responsible for keeping records and accounts, for giving advice on budgets to other departments, and for paying wages and salaries.
HUMAN RESOURCES	This department deals with the recruitment of new staff, the training of new and existing staff, pay negotiations and regular staff appraisals.

Activity 16

Switch the computer off	
Use the screen lock facility to lock the computer screen	✔
Stay at your desk	
Put some papers over the screen to hide the information from passers by	

Activity 17

Confidentiality	✔
Flexibility	
Integrity	✔
Confidence	
Numeracy	

Activity 18

Offering free lunches for staff	
Training staff to use the recycling facilities	✔
Keeping the computers switched on at all times	
Using video conferencing instead of travelling to customers' premises	✔

Essential accounting terminology

2

Introduction

The purpose of accounting is to be able to provide financial information about an organisation. For example, managers will want to keep track of the profit made by the organisation in a certain period, and they will also want to see how much the organisation is worth at a specific point in time.

To be able to provide this information it is important that the business transactions of the organisation are recorded and summarised into accounting records.

This chapter will introduce you to the accounting terminology used to record these business transactions.

KNOWLEDGE	CONTENTS
Introduction to Bookkeeping	1 Assets
3 Know the terminology used in bookkeeping	2 Liabilities
	3 Income and expenditure
Working within Bookkeeping	4 Cash and credit transactions
3 Understand what is meant by both cash and credit transactions	5 Profit and loss
	6 Summary and further questions

1 Assets

1.1 What is an asset?

Assets are items of value which an organisation owns in order to generate profit by selling goods or providing a service.

1.2 Different types of asset

 Examples

Assets include:

Premises – organisations usually need a building from which to carry out their business. These premises could be an office building, a shop, or a factory.

Fixtures and fittings – these are items in the premises which are used to provide goods or services. For example, the computers in an office, the shelving in a shop, or machinery in a factory.

Vehicles – vehicles may be needed to deliver goods or provide a service to customers.

Stock – goods which are ready to sell to customers are kept in stock

Bank – the funds available in the organisation's bank account may be used to purchase more stock to sell.

Cash – some organisations keep money on the premises so that they can buy small items.

Debtors – amounts owed to the organisation by customers as a result of sales made on credit.

1.3 Definition

 Definition

An 'asset' is an item of value owned by an organisation.

2 Liabilities

2.1 What is a liability?

Liabilities are debts owed by the organisation. The money will usually have been used to buy assets for the organisation to use.

Total liabilities are deducted from total assets to calculate an organisation's worth at a specific period in time.

2.2 Different types of liability

 Examples

Liabilities include:

Creditors – amounts owed by the organisation to suppliers of goods and services.

Bank Overdraft – an arrangement that allows an organisation to take more money out of its bank than it has put in. The money is owed to the bank.

Bank Loan – a fixed amount of money an organisation borrows from the bank.

2.3 Definition

 Definition

A 'liability' is a debt owed by an organisation to other organisations, businesses and individuals.

3 Income and expenditure

3.1 Introduction

The purpose of most organisations is to make a profit or to raise funds so that they can continue supplying goods and services to customers. To calculate profit, **expenditure** is deducted from **income**.

3.2 What is income?

Any money received from the supply of goods and services to customers is known as income.

3.3 What is expenditure?

Any money paid for purchasing the goods and services and day to day expenses is known as expenditure.

 Definitions

Income is the money received by an organisation from selling its goods and services.

Expenditure is the money paid by an organisation to purchase goods and services.

 Activity 1

Which of the following items are assets, liabilities, income or expenditure? Put a tick in the correct box.

	Asset	Liability	Income	Expenditure
Creditors				
Electricity bill				
Money in the bank				
Bank overdraft				
Sales to customers				
Debtors				
Office computers				

4 Cash and Credit Transactions

4.1 Recording cash and credit transactions

Income is the amount of money received by an organisation from its sales. Sometimes this money is received immediately and sometimes the money is paid later. It is important that these cash and credit transactions are recorded separately so that the organisation knows how much money it is owed by customers, and how much it owes to suppliers.

4.2 Cash and credit sales

 Definitions

Sales is the exchange of goods or services to an individual or organisation in exchange for money.

A **customer** is an individual or organisation to whom the goods or services have been sold. The organisation supplying the goods or services will then receive money in exchange.

A **debtor** is a customer who has been sold goods on credit.

Cash Sales is the term used to describe a payment at point of sale. The payment itself can be made by cash (currency), cheque, debit or credit card, or bank transfer. An example of a cash sale is when you go into a shop, choose the items you want to buy, and pay for them immediately.

Credit Sales are sales made where the goods or services will be paid later than the point of sale. Many organisations give credit to their regular trade customers so that one payment can be made for all the transactions made in each month.

4.3 Cash and credit customers

With cash sales the organisation gets the money immediately from the customer and the relationship ends there. With credit customers, there is a risk to the organisation that the customer may not pay for the goods. Therefore, before allowing customers to pay on credit the organisation will make certain checks to ensure that the customer can pay.

It is assumed that the money owed by credit customers will be paid and therefore they are classed as debtors (assets) of the organisation.

4.4   Cash and credit purchases

 Definition

Purchases – to buy goods or services from an organisation in exchange for money.

Cash Purchases are when goods or services are paid for at the time of purchase.

A florist may purchase some stock and pay by 'cash'. Although the payment could be by cash (currency), credit card or debit card or bank transfer, if the payment is made immediately it is classed as a cash purchase.

Credit Purchases are when an organisation pays for the goods or services sometime after making the purchase. The money will be sent to the supplier after an agreed amount of time, for example, thirty days.

The supplier is now a creditor (liability) of the organisation.

 Definition

A **supplier** is an individual or organisation providing goods or services to another in exchange for money.

A **creditor** is a supplier who is owed money for goods purchased on credit.

4.5   The Cash Book and Petty Cash Book

The word 'cash' is also used in accounting as a name for recording monetary transactions.

A **Cash Book** is used to keep a record of most of the receipts and payments made by the organisation. The actual monies received and recorded may be by cash (currency), cheque, credit card or debit card, or bank transfer.

A **Petty Cash Book** is used to record the small amount of cash that most businesses hold in order to make small cash payments regularly. Petty cash systems and the management of petty cash are addressed further later in this book.

Activity 2

C Froome's Cycle World

Mr Froome has a small shop selling and repairing bicycles for individual customers.

He buys the spare parts that he needs from a large wholesaler.

Do you think that Mr Froome's income comes from cash sales or credit sales?

Do you think that the expenditure for spare parts is cash purchases or credit purchases?

5 Profit and loss

5.1 Profit and Loss

Organisations need to keep a careful record of their income from sales and their expenditure so that they can calculate if the company has made a profit or a loss.

Profit is the amount of money an organisation earns after expenditure has been deducted from income.

Loss is when an organisation has spent more money than it has earned from income.

5.2 Types of profit

There are two types of profit you will need to know about for this unit.

Gross profit is a very important figure. It can be used as a comparison to see how well the business is doing compared to other businesses, or if it is doing better or worse than in previous years.

To calculate gross profit, the cost of goods sold (purchases) is deducted from income.

Net profit is calculated by deducting all other expenses from gross profit. These other expenses could include wages, rent and rates and other property expenses, and costs for running vehicles. The net profit will show whether a company has covered all its expenses with the income that it has generated.

5.3 Gross profit and net profit calculations

INCOME

From Cash and Credit sales

less

COST OF SALES

The cost of purchasing the goods which have been sold

equals

GROSS PROFIT

less

EXPENSES

Everyday running costs such as wages, lighting, heating, office expenses, etc.

equals

NET PROFIT or LOSS

 Example 1

Your organisation has recorded all sales income and expenditure for the previous month. You have been asked to calculate the gross and net profit for the month.

	£
Sales income from cash and credit sales	125,000
Cost of sales	75,000
Wages	15,000
Premises expenses	3,000
Vehicle expenses	2,500

Solution:

To calculate **gross profit** the cost of sales are deducted from the sales income.

Sales income:	£125,000
– Cost of sales:	-£ 75,000
= Gross profit:	£ 50,000

To calculate **net profit** all other expenses are deducted from the gross profit.

First you will need to add up all the other expenses: wages, premises expenses, vehicle expenses to find total expenditure.

Wages:	£	15,000
+ Premises expenses:	£	3,000
+ Vehicle expenses:	£	2,500
= Total expenditure:	£	20,500

Then, you need to deduct the total expenditure from gross profit.

Gross Profit:	£ 50,000
-Total expenditure:	-£ 20,500
= Net Profit:	£ 29,500

 Example 2

For the previous month, a business has recorded income of £82,000. The cost of those sales was £66,000 and the other expenses were £25,000. Has the business made a profit or a loss?

Answer: *The business has made a gross profit of £16,000. However, after deducting the remaining expenses of £25,000, the business has made a Net Loss of £9,000.*

 Activity 3

Your organisation has recorded all sales income and expenditure for the previous month. You have been asked to calculate the gross and net profit for the month.

	£
Sales income from cash and credit sales	78,000
Cost of sales	50,700
Wages	7,500
Premises expenses	1,750
Vehicle expenses	2,000

a) Calculate the gross profit for the month

b) Calculate the net profit or loss for the month

Activity 4

An organisation has total income lower than costs of sales plus expenses. Has the organisation made a profit or a loss?

6 Summary and further questions

This chapter has introduced you to some important accounting terminology. You can distinguish between assets, liabilities, income and expenditure. You have also looked at the difference between credit sales and purchases and cash sales and purchases. Finally, the chapter looked at the two different types of profit that an organisation needs to consider.

The further practice questions below test your knowledge of this key terminology.

 Activity 5

Match the definition with the correct term.

Terms	Definition
Creditor	Something the business owns
Debtor	A person or another business that the organisation owes money to
Asset	Something the business owes
Liability	A person or another business that owes money to the organisation

 Activity 6

Fill in the gaps below to complete the sentences. Choose from the Pick list provided.

When an organisation pays for items of expenditure at the time of purchase this is known as a _____

When an organisation allows a customer to pay the amount they owe at a later date this is known as a _____

Pick List

credit sale   cash sale   cash purchase   credit purchase.

KAPLAN PUBLISHING

Activity 7

Choose the correct option in each of these statements

a. The sum of money spent in making sales is known as [sales/cost of sales]

b. If total income is greater than the cost of sales plus other expenses the organisation has made a [profit/loss]

c. If total income is less than the cost of sales plus other expenses the organisation has made a [profit/loss]

d. Sales income less cost of sales equals [gross profit/net profit]

 Activity 8

Which of the following items are cash or credit sales, or cash or credit purchases? Put a tick in the correct box.

	Cash Sale	Credit Sale	Cash Purchase	Credit Purchase
Goods bought from a supplier and paid for immediately.				
Goods delivered to a customer who will pay at the end of the month.				
Items bought from a supplier on credit.				
A payment received from a customer for goods purchased in the shop and paid for at the till.				

Activity 9

Last year your organisation recorded income and expenditure in the table below

Income and Expenditure	£
Sales	156,000
Cost of Sales	93,600
Wages	21,060
Administration Expenses	18,720
Selling Expenses	12,844

Use the income and expenditure figures to complete the following calculations:

Calculate Gross Profit   £ [   ]

Calculate Net Profit   £ [   ]

Activity 10

Last year your organisation recorded income and expenditure in the table below

Income and Expenditure	£
Sales	152,880
Cost of Sales	91,728
Wages	20,640
Administration Expenses	18,350
Selling Expenses	12,590

Use the income and expenditure figures to complete the following calculations:

Calculate Gross Profit   £ [   ]

Calculate Net Profit   £ [   ]

Answers to chapter activities

Activity 1

	Asset	Liability	Income	Expenditure
Creditors		✓		
Electricity bill				✓
Money in the bank	✓			
Bank overdraft		✓		
Sales to customers			✓	
Debtors	✓			
Office computers	✓			

Activity 2

Mr Froome's income is most likely to be from cash sales. His customers are individuals who will probably pay when they come to pick up their bicycles. They are unlikely to be very regular customers.

His expenditure for the spare parts is likely to be a credit purchase. As Mr Froome will buy regularly from the supplier he may have been given credit so that he can make daily or weekly purchases and then pay for all he owes at a later date.

Activity 3

a) The gross profit for the month is £27,300 (£78,000 - £50,700)

b) The net profit for the month is £16,050 (£27,300 – (£7,500+£1,750+£2,000))

Activity 4

As income is lower than cost of sales plus expenses, the business has made a loss.

Activity 5

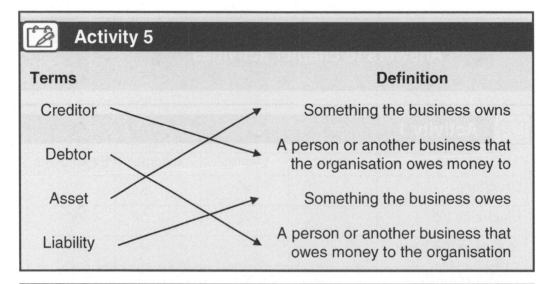

Terms	Definition
Creditor	Something the business owns
Debtor	A person or another business that the organisation owes money to
Asset	Something the business owes
Liability	A person or another business that owes money to the organisation

 Activity 6

When an organisation pays for items of expenditure at the time of purchase this is known as a **cash purchase.**

When an organisation allows a customer to pay the amount they owe at a later date this is known as a **credit sale.**

Activity 7

a. The sum of money spent in making sales is known as [**cost of sales**]

b. If total income is greater than the cost of sales plus other expenses the organisation has made a [**profit**]

c. If total income is less than the cost of sales plus other expenses the organisation has made a [**loss**]

d. Sales income less cost of sales equals [**gross profit**]

KAPLAN PUBLISHING

Activity 8

Which of the following items are cash or credit sales, or cash or credit purchases? Put a tick in the correct box.

	Cash Sale	Credit Sale	Cash Purchase	Credit Purchase
Goods bought from a supplier and paid for immediately.			√	
Goods delivered to a customer who will pay at the end of the month.		√		
Items bought from a supplier on credit.				√
A payment received from a customer for goods purchased in the shop and paid for at the till.	√			

 Activity 9

Last year your organisation recorded income and expenditure in the table below

Income and Expenditure	£
Sales	156,000
Cost of Sales	93,600
Wages	21,060
Administration Expenses	18,720
Selling Expenses	12,844

Use the income and expenditure figures to complete the following calculations:

Calculate Gross Profit £ 62,400

Calculate Net Profit £ 9,776

Activity 10

Last year your organisation recorded income and expenditure in the table below

Income and Expenditure	£
Sales	152,880
Cost of Sales	91,728
Wages	20,640
Administration Expenses	18,350
Selling Expenses	12,590

Use the income and expenditure figures to complete the following calculations:

Calculate Gross Profit   £   61,152

Calculate Net Profit   £   9,572

Business documents for accounting transactions

Introduction

As we have already seen, it is important that customer and supplier transactions are recorded separately so that organisations know how much money they are owed by customers, and how much they owe to suppliers.

Business documents are used to record these transactions and the documents are exchanged between the supplier and the customer so that both parties have a record of each transaction. It is important that both the supplier and the customer keep a copy of each of these documents. Mistakes can happen and each document is proof of each stage of the transaction.

The name of a transaction or document will depend on whether we look at it from the point of view of the seller or the purchaser. Thus an invoice may be called a 'sales invoice' for the seller but a 'purchase invoice' for the purchaser, although it is the same document. Similarly, the same transaction is called a 'sale' by the supplier and a 'purchase' by the customer.

KNOWLEDGE	CONTENTS
Bookkeeping and accounts 1 Know how to complete financial documents **Working within bookkeeping** 2 Know the general principles of VAT 4 Understand the principles of coding and batch control	1 Documents used to record credit transactions 2 Documents used to record cash transactions 3 Using codes 4 Summary

1 Documents used to record credit transactions

1.1 Introduction

This chapter reviews the main documents involved in the flow of business transactions.

1.2 Offering credit and price quotations

Most transactions between business organisations will be on credit terms and this involves an element of risk. The goods are being taken away or delivered to the customer now with the promise of payment in the future. Therefore, suppliers must be confident that payment will be received.

In some organisations it is common practice to quote prices to customers over the telephone particularly if there is a catalogue or price list from which there are no deviations in price. However, some businesses will be prepared to offer certain customers goods at different prices and discounts may be offered and/or given to customers. Therefore, it is often the case that a price quotation is sent to a customer showing the price at which the goods that they want can be bought. The customer can then decide whether or not to buy the goods at that price.

1.3 Purchase Order

If the customer is happy with the price quotation that they have received from the supplier then they will place a purchase order for the goods or services required.

This document will state the details of the goods required, including:

- the quantity and description of the goods
- the price and other terms
- the supplier's code number for the items
- the date the order was placed.

When the supplier receives a purchase order, it is important for them to check all of the details carefully as it forms part of the sales contract.

- Is the price that which was quoted to the customer?
- Are the delivery terms acceptable?
- Are any discounts applicable?

KAPLAN PUBLISHING

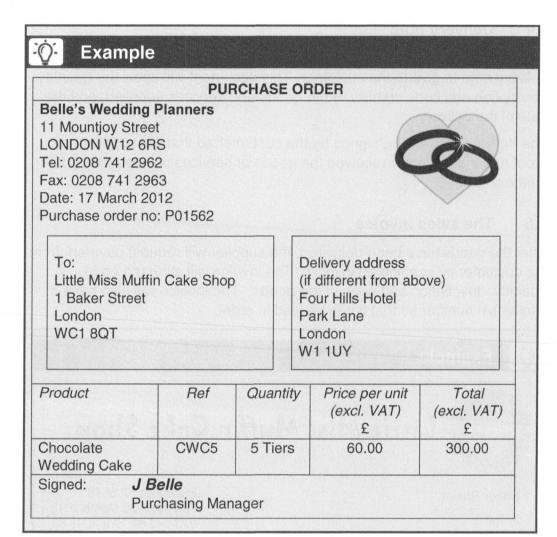

Example

PURCHASE ORDER				
Belle's Wedding Planners 11 Mountjoy Street LONDON W12 6RS Tel: 0208 741 2962 Fax: 0208 741 2963 Date: 17 March 2012 Purchase order no: P01562				
To: Little Miss Muffin Cake Shop 1 Baker Street London WC1 8QT		Delivery address (if different from above) Four Hills Hotel Park Lane London W1 1UY		

Product	Ref	Quantity	Price per unit (excl. VAT) £	Total (excl. VAT) £
Chocolate Wedding Cake	CWC5	5 Tiers	60.00	300.00
Signed: **J Belle** Purchasing Manager				

Notes:

a) The customer, Belle's Wedding Supplies has placed an order with the supplier of the cakes, Little Miss Muffin Cake Shop.

b) The purchase order clearly states that the customer wants to purchase 5 tiers of chocolate wedding cake at a price of £60.00 for each tier.

c) The total amount that the customer wants to pay for the cake is £300.00 (5 tiers x £60.00 = £300.00).

d) If Little Miss Muffin Cake Shop does not agree with any of these details they will need to contact Belle's Wedding Supplies immediately. The purchase order has been signed by J Belle, the authorised signatory.

Definitions

An **authorised signatory** is an individual who has been given permission to sign an official document on behalf of the organisation.

1.4 Delivery note

When the goods or services are supplied, the supplier will prepare a delivery note to give to the customer. This document will show the quantity, description and code number of the goods and services supplied; and the date of the delivery.

The delivery note will be signed by the customer so that the supplier has proof that the customer received the goods or services, in case of any later queries.

1.5 The sales invoice

After the goods have been delivered, the supplier will request payment from the customer by sending an invoice. The invoice will state the code, quantity, description and price of the goods. The invoice will also have a sequential number so that it can be filed in order.

 Example

 Little Miss Muffin Cake Shop

1 Baker Street
London
WC1 8QT
Tel: 020 7890 1234 – Fax: 020 7890 1235

Invoice no: 005673
Tax point: 25 March 2012
VAT reg no: 618 2201 63
Delivery note: DN00673
Account no: BEL65

INVOICE

To:
Belle's Wedding Planners
11 Mountjoy St
London W12 6RS

Delivery:
Four Hills Hotel
Park Lane
London W1 1UY

Delivery date:
25 March 2012

Date: 25 March 2012

Sales order number: 41161

Product	Quantity	Price per unit (£)	Total (£)
Chocolate Wedding Cake	5 tiers	60.00	300.00
		VAT 20%	60.00
		Total	360.00
Payment terms: 14 days net			

Notes

This invoice confirms the price of the goods supplied to the customer

a) 5 Tiers of wedding cake which have been supplied to the Belle's.

b) The price for the goods is £300.

c) Value Added Tax (VAT) of 20%, £60.00 has been added to the cost of the goods.

d) The amount of £360.00 is now due from the customer.

e) The payment is due in 14 days from the date of the invoice.

1.6 Pricing and discounts

Unit prices for goods or services are kept in master files which must be updated regularly. If a price quotation has been sent to a customer then this must be used to determine the price to use on the invoice.

Trade discounts are a definite amount that is deducted from the list price of the goods for the supplies to some customers, with the intention of encouraging and rewarding customer loyalty. As well as checking the actual calculation of the trade discount on the face of the invoice, the supplier's file or the price quotation should be checked to ensure that the correct percentage of trade discount has been deducted.

Even if no trade discount appears on the purchase invoice, the supplier's file or price quotation must still be checked as it may be that a trade discount should have been deducted.

A **bulk discount** is similar to a trade discount in that it is deducted from the list price on the invoice. However, a bulk discount is given by a supplier for orders above a certain size.

A **settlement discount** is offered to customers if they settle the invoice within a certain time period. The discount is expressed as a percentage of the invoice total but is not deducted from the invoice total as it is not certain whether or not it will be accepted. Instead the details of the settlement discount will be noted at the bottom of the invoice.

1.7 The impact of VAT (sales tax)

Sales tax (VAT) is a tax levied on consumer expenditure. The procedure is that it is collected at each stage in the production and distribution chain.

Prices will normally be quoted exclusive of value added tax (VAT), as this is the true selling price to the business. However, if the selling business is registered for VAT, VAT must be charged on taxable supplies.

Most businesses avoid having to treat VAT as an expense as they may deduct the VAT (sales tax) they have paid on their purchases **(input tax)** from the VAT (sales tax) they charge to customers on their sales **(output tax)** and pay only the difference to the tax authorities.

Let us look at a simple illustration. We will assume a standard rate of 20%, and follow one article, a wooden table, through the production and distribution chain.

- A private individual cuts down a tree and sells it to a timber mill for £10. **Tax effect** – none. The individual is not a taxable person in this case.

- The timber mill saws the log and sells the timber to a furniture manufacturer for £100 + VAT.

  Tax effect – Being a taxable person, the mill is obliged to charge its customers VAT at 20% on the selling price (output tax).

  Cash effect – The mill collected £120 from the customer (or has a receivable for this sum). Of this, £20 has to be paid to the tax authorities (HM Revenue and Customs), and therefore only £100 would be recognised as sales.

- The manufacturer makes a table from the wood, and sells this to a retailer for £400 + VAT.

  Tax effect – The manufacturer is obliged to charge VAT at 20% on the selling price (i.e. £80 output tax), but in this instance would be allowed to reduce this amount by setting off the input tax of £20 charged on the purchase of wood from the mill.

  Cash effect – Tax of £60 is paid to the tax authorities (HM Revenue and Customs) (output less input tax = £80 less £20). £400 is recognised as sales and £100 as purchases in the accounts.

- The retailer sells the table to a private customer for £1,000 plus VAT of £200. **Tax effect** – The retailer charges £200 of VAT to the customer but against this output tax may be set off the input tax of £80 charged on the purchase from the manufacturer.

  Cash effect – £120 (£200 – £80) is paid to the tax authorities (HM Revenue and Customs). Purchases would be shown in the books at £400 and sales at £1,000.

- **The private customer** – VAT is a tax levied on consumer expenditure and the chain ends here. The customer is not a taxable person, and cannot recover the tax paid.

KAPLAN PUBLISHING

You will note that everybody else has passed the sales on and, though the customer has paid his £200 to the retailer, the tax authorities (HM Revenue and Customs) has received its tax by contributions from each link in the chain, as shown below:

	£
Timber mill	20.00
Manufacturer	60.00
Retailer	120.00
	———
	200.00
	———

🔍 Definitions

Sales tax (VAT) is charged on the **taxable supply of goods and services** in the United Kingdom by a **taxable person** in the course of a business carried on by him.

Output tax is the tax charged on the sale of goods and services.

Input tax is the tax paid on the purchase of goods and services.

1.8 Rates of VAT (sales tax)

Taxable supply is the supply of all items except those which are **exempt.** Examples of exempt items are as follows:

- certain land and buildings, where sold, leased or hired
- insurance
- postal services

Input tax cannot be reclaimed where the trader's supplies are all exempt.

There are three rates of sales tax (VAT in the UK) on taxable supplies:

1. Some items are 'zero-rated' (similar to exempt except that input tax can be reclaimed), examples of which include:

    - water and most types of food
    - books and newspapers
    - drugs and medicines
    - children's clothing and footwear.

2. There is a special rate of 5% for domestic fuel and power

3. All other items are rated at the standard rate of 20%.

VAT on some items is non-deductible. This means that VAT on any purchases of these items cannot be deducted from the amount of tax payable to the tax authorities (HM Revenue and Customs). The business has to bear the VAT as an expense. Non-deductible items include motor cars and business entertaining.

For our purposes you will normally be dealing with taxable supplies at the standard rate of 20%.

Therefore, if you are given the net price of goods, the price excluding VAT, then the amount of VAT is 20/100 of this price.

Note, VAT is always rounded down to the nearest penny.

 Example

A sale is made for £360.48 plus VAT. What is the amount of VAT to be charged on this sale?

Solution

VAT = £360.48 × 20/100 = £72.09

Remember to round down to the nearest penny.

An alternative way of calculating this would to be to multiply the net amount of £360.48 by 20%.

If a price is given that already includes the VAT then calculating the VAT requires an understanding of the price structure where VAT is concerned.

	%
Selling price incl. VAT (gross)	120
VAT	20
	___
Selling price excl. VAT (net)	100
	___

 Example

Goods have a selling price of £3,000 inclusive of VAT. What is the VAT on the goods and the net price of these goods?

Solution

	£
Net price (£3,000× 100/120)	2,500
VAT (£3,000 × 20/120)	500
	___
Gross price	3,000
	___

1.9 VAT and discounts

When a settlement discount is offered, this makes the VAT calculation slightly more complex.

Invoices should show the VAT payable as 20% (or whichever rate of sales tax is applicable) of the **discounted price**. The amount of VAT paid is always based on the discounted amount even though when the invoice is being prepared it is not known whether the customer will or will not take advantage of the settlement discount.

 Activity 1

What is the amount of VAT on each of the following transactions?

i)   £100 net of VAT
ii)   £250 net of VAT
iii) £480 including VAT
iv)   £600 including VAT
v)   A sale of £280.00 plus VAT with a settlement discount of 2%

1.10 Preparing a sales invoice

 Example

Thelma Goody is the sales invoicing clerk for a VAT registered clothing wholesaler. Thelma prepares the sales invoices to be sent to the customer from the price list and a copy of the delivery note sent up to her by the sales department. Today she has received the following delivery note from the sales department.

Delivery note: 2685

To: K Clothes Ltd
9 Port Street
MANCHESTER
M1 5EX

A B Fashions Ltd
3 Park Road
Parkway
Bristol
BR6 6SJ
Tel: 01272 695221
Fax: 01272 695222

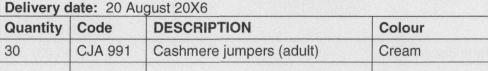

Delivery date: 20 August 20X6

Quantity	Code	DESCRIPTION	Colour
30	CJA 991	Cashmere jumpers (adult)	Cream

Received by: ....

Signature: .... Date: ....

Code	Description	Colour	Unit price	VAT rate
CJA 991	Cashmere jumper (adult)	Cream	65.00	Standard
CJA 992	Cashmere jumper (adult)	Pink	65.00	Standard
CJA 993	Cashmere jumper (adult)	Blue	65.00	Standard
CJA 994	Cashmere jumper (adult)	Camel	65.00	Standard

The customer file shows that K Clothes Ltd's account number is KC 0055 and that a trade discount of 10% is offered to this customer.

Thelma must now prepare the sales invoice. Today's date is 22 August 20X6.

Solution

INVOICE

Invoice to:
K Clothes Ltd
9 Port Street
MANCHESTER
M1 5EX

A B Fashions Ltd
3 Park Road
Parkway
Bristol
BR6 6SJ
Tel: 01272 695221
Fax: 01272 695222

Deliver to:

As above

Invoice no:	95124
Tax point:	22 August 20X6
VAT reg no:	488 7922 26
Delivery note no:	2685
Account no:	KC 0055

Code	Description	Quantity	VAT rate %	Unit price £	Amount excl of VAT £
CJA 991	Cashmere jumper (adult) cream	30	20	65.00	1,950.00
					1,950.00
Trade discount 10%					(195.00)
					1,755.00
VAT					351.00
Total amount payable					2,106.00

How did Thelma do it?

Step 1   Enter today's date on the invoice and the invoice number which should be the next number after the last sales invoice number.

Step 2   Enter the customer details – name, address and account number.

Step 3   Refer now to the delivery note copy and enter the delivery note number and the quantities, codes and descriptions of the goods.

Step 4   Refer to the price list and enter the unit prices of the goods and the rate of VAT

Step 5   Now for the calculations – firstly multiply the number of each item by the unit price to find the VAT exclusive price – then total these total prices – finally calculate the trade discount as 10% of this total, £1,950.00 × 10% = £195.00 and deduct it.

Step 6   Calculate the VAT – in this case there is only standard rate VAT on the cashmere jumpers but you must remember to deduct the trade discount (£1,950 – £195) before calculating the VAT amount £1,755 × 20% = £351 – add the VAT to the invoice total after deducting the trade discount.

1.11   Credit Notes

In some cases, the customer may want to return goods to the supplier. For example, if the goods are faulty. When this happens, the supplier will issue a credit note. This credit note will reduce the amount that the customer owes.

Common reasons for credit notes:

- when a customer has returned faulty or damaged goods
- when a customer has returned perfect goods by agreement with the supplier
- to make a refund for short deliveries
- to settle a dispute with a customer.

When a supplier receives returned goods they must be inspected, counted and recorded on receipt. They would normally be recorded on a returns inwards note.

All credit notes must be authorised by a supervisor prior to being issued to the customer.

Some credit notes may be issued without a returns inwards note. For example, an error may have been made in pricing on an invoice but the customer is satisfied with the goods and does not need to return them.

These credit notes must be issued only after written authorisation has been received and must be reviewed and approved before being sent to the customer or recorded.

As credit notes look very similar to invoices, they are often printed in red to make it clear that it is not an invoice.

 Example

 Little Miss Muffin Cake Shop

1 Baker Street	Credit note no: CN 02542
London	Tax point: 30 March 2012
WC1 8QT	VAT reg no: 618 2201 63
Tel: 020 7890 1234 – Fax: 020 7890 1235	Invoice no: 005673
	Account no: BEL65

CREDIT NOTE

Credit to:
Belle's Wedding Planners
11 Mountjoy St
London W12 6RS

Date: 30 March 2012

Description	Code	Quantity	Unit price £	Amount exclusive of VAT £
Chocolate Wedding Cake	CWC5	1 tier	60.00	60.00
VAT				12.00
Total amount of credit				72.00

Reason: One tier burnt.

Notes

In this example, one of the tiers of the cake was burnt, so Belle's Wedding Supplies have requested a credit note.

When the replacement tier has been made and delivered, Little Miss Muffin Cake Shop will raise another invoice for the replacement tier.

1.12   Statement of Account

At the end of each month, the supplier will summarise all the transactions that have taken place with the customer. This could include invoices, credit notes, and any payments received from the customer.

The statement of account will show the outstanding balance owing from the customer at the end of the month.

 Example

 Little Miss Muffin Cake Shop

1 Baker Street

London

WC1 8QT

Tel: 020 7890 1234 – Fax: 020 7890 1235

STATEMENT

To: Belle's Wedding Planners
Date: 31 March 2012

Date	Transaction	Debit £	Credit £	Balance £
1 March	Balance b/d	165.00		165.00
25 March	Invoice 5673	360.00		525.00
30 March	Credit Note 02452		72.00	453.00
31 March	Cash received		165.00	288.00

Notes

a)   1st March   Belle's Wedding Planners owed £165.00 from last month;

b)   25th March   Invoice No 5673 for £360.00 has been added to the £165.00 to show a balance owing of £525.00;

c)   30th March   Credit note No 02452 for £72.00 has been deducted from the £525.00 to show a balance at that date of £453.00;

d)   31st March   Belle's Wedding Planners have paid the amount owing at the beginning of the month, leaving a balance outstanding of £288.00.

1.13   Remittance Advice

The final document in the process is the remittance advice. When the customer pays their outstanding balance they will send a remittance advice to the supplier together with their payment.

The remittance advice will clearly show which invoices are being paid and the date of the payment.

If there are any credit notes, the customer will state which credit notes they are deducting from the payment.

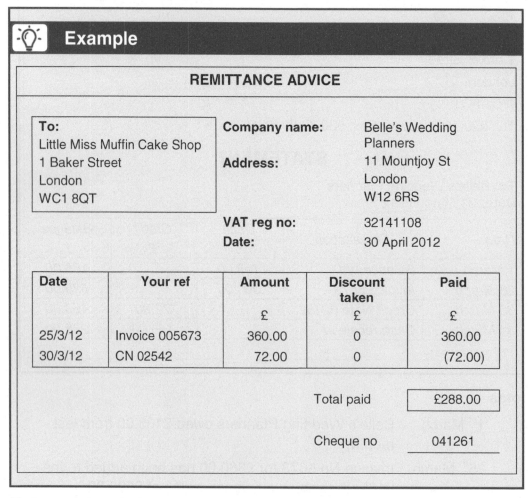

Example

REMITTANCE ADVICE

To:	Company name:	Belle's Wedding Planners
Little Miss Muffin Cake Shop		
1 Baker Street	Address:	11 Mountjoy St
London		London
WC1 8QT		W12 6RS
	VAT reg no:	32141108
	Date:	30 April 2012

Date	Your ref	Amount	Discount taken	Paid
		£	£	£
25/3/12	Invoice 005673	360.00	0	360.00
30/3/12	CN 02542	72.00	0	(72.00)

	Total paid	£288.00
	Cheque no	041261

Notes

In this example, on 30th April, 2012, Belle's Wedding Planners paid £288.00 by cheque. This payment is £360.00 for Invoice No 005673 less £72.00 for Credit Note CN02542.

If customers do not send a remittance advice and there are a lot of transactions in the month, it would be difficult for the supplier to know which invoices and credit notes the payment relates to.

1.14 Overview of the flow of transaction

The diagram below shows the typical flow of a transaction including the documents involved.

Dependent on whether it is a credit sale or a credit purchase, we will be looking at it from the perspective of the business or customer.

Customer	Supplier
Purchase order ⟶	
⟵	Sends *delivery note* with
	goods supplied
Signs delivery note ⟶	
⟵	Sends *invoice*
Returns goods ⟶	
⟵	Sends *credit note*
⟵	Sends *statement of account*
	(usually on a monthly basis)
Sends *remittance advice* ⟶	
with payment	

Activity 2

Which two documents are sent by the customer to the supplier?

Activity 3

Which documents are sent by the supplier to the customer?

2 Documents used to record cash transactions

2.1 Receipt

In a cash sale or purchase, the transaction is much simpler. The customer will probably place an order verbally and payment is always made as soon as the customer receives the goods or services.

The customer will need a copy of the sales receipt in case they need to return them to the supplier.

3 Using codes

3.1 Common systems of codes

To be able to find and process the information quickly and efficiently, abbreviations or codes are often used.

Common systems of codes are:

Alphabetical codes

Codes which are made up of a series of letters only. These are short forms of a full title. For example:

Code   Description

AAT   Association of Accounting Technicians

ACS   AAT Access

Numerical codes

Codes which are made up of a series of numbers only. For example, a sequential list of invoice numbers.

4156

4157

4158

Alphanumerical codes

These codes are a mixture of letters and numbers. Alphanumerical codes are often used for customer and supplier codes. For example:

BEL65	Belle's Wedding Planners
FRO02	Froome's Bicycle Repairs
CIR01	Ciro's Light Bites & Nibbles

 Activity 4

Draw a line to match the Code provided with the Type of Code which best describes it.

Code	Type of Code
PAP113	Numerical
KAPL	Alphanumeric
006786	Alphabetical

---

4 Summary and further questions

In this chapter you looked in detail at the documents used to record transactions for credit and cash customers.

You also looked at how codes can be used to process information efficiently and effectively.

Business documents for accounting transactions: **Chapter 3**

Activity 5

Organisations issue and receive different documents when buying and selling goods.

Draw a line to match the document with the transaction

Transaction	Document
A document sent by the supplier to the customer listing the goods or services supplied and requesting payment	Purchase Order
A document sent by the supplier to inform the customer of any amounts refunded following the return of goods or errors on a previous invoice.	Invoice
A document sent by the customer to inform the supplier that an invoice has been paid.	Credit Note
A document sent to a supplier detailing the goods that the customer wants to purchase.	Statement of Account
A document that summarises the transactions between a supplier and customer. It shows the invoices and credit notes sent, payments received and any outstanding balance on the account.	Remittance Advice

Activity 6

Your organisation purchased 24 boxes of paper towels at £12.45 for each box. What is the total of the paper towels?

£ [   ]

Activity 7

You work for Posies and Roses Florists. A customer purchased 24 red roses at £1.75 each. What is the total cost?

£ [   ]

KAPLAN PUBLISHING

Activity 8

The customer who purchased the roses in Activity 7 has complained that 4 of the roses are damaged. Unfortunately, there are no more roses available so the manager has agreed to issue a credit note. How much does the customer owe after the credit note has been issued?

£ [   ]

Activity 9

You work for Cavalier Beds as a sales invoicing clerk. Your task is to prepare a sales invoice for each customer using the information below.

Today is 28 October, 20X6 and you have received the following delivery note from the sales department.

Use the information from the delivery note, the information from the customer file and the price list below to prepare an invoice for KP Furniture Ltd.

The last invoice issued was Invoice No. 67894.

Delivery Note:

Delivery note: 6785

To: KP Furniture Ltd
9 Paris Street
COLCHESTER
CF25 1XY

Cavalier Beds
3 Brussels Road
County Road
Gloucester
GL6 6TH
Tel: 01456 698271
Fax: 01456 698272

Delivery date: 27 October 20X6

Quantity	Code	DESCRIPTION	Size
5	MAT15K	Deluxe Mattress	King Size

Received by: ....

Signature: .... Date: ....

Customer File:

The customer file shows that KP Furniture Ltd's account number is KP12 and a trade discount of 10% is offered to this customer.

Price List:

Code	Description	Size	Unit price	VAT rate
MAT15S	Deluxe Mattress	Single	58.00	Standard
MAT15D	Deluxe Mattress	Double	74.00	Standard
MAT15K	Deluxe Mattress	King	98.00	Standard

Cavalier Beds
3 Brussels Road
County Road
Gloucester
GL6 6TH
Tel: 01456 698271   Fax: 01456 698272

Invoice to:

Invoice no:	
Date:	
VAT reg no:	488 7922 26
Delivery note no:	
Account no:	

Code		Quantity	VAT rate	Unit price £	Amount excl of VAT £
			20%	£	
Trade discount 10%					
Subtotal					
VAT					
Total amount payable					

Activity 10

A customer has been sent two invoices totalling £457.98 and £69.65. They have also received a credit note for goods returned to the supplier. This credit note was for a total of £58.60. During the month, the customer paid £200.00 to the supplier.

a) What is the balance outstanding on this customer's account?

£ [   ]

b) What is the name of the document which will be sent to the customer to show these transactions and the balance outstanding?

[   ]

Answers to chapter activities

Activity 1

i)	£100.00 × 20/100	=	£20.00
ii)	£250.00 × 20/100	=	£50.00
iii)	£480.00 × 20/120	=	£80.00
iv)	£600.00 × 20/120	=	£100.00
v)	£(280 – 2% x 280) x 20/100 = £54.88		

Activity 2

The customer sends a **purchase order** to state which goods they want to purchase and a **remittance advice** to say which transactions they are paying.

Activity 3

The supplier sends a **delivery note** with the goods when they are supplied; an **invoice** to tell the customer how much the goods cost; and a **statement of account** to summarise all the transactions that have taken place.

Activity 4

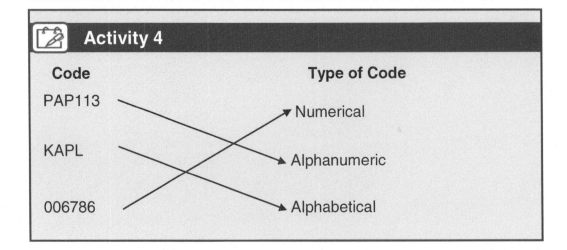

KAPLAN PUBLISHING

Activity 5

Transaction	Document
A document sent by the supplier to the customer listing the goods or services supplied and requesting payment	Purchase Order
A document sent by the supplier to inform the customer of any amounts refunded following the return of goods or errors on a previous invoice.	Invoice
A document sent by the customer to inform the supplier that an invoice has been paid.	Credit Note
A document sent to a supplier detailing the goods that the customer wants to purchase.	Statement of Account
A document that summarises the transactions between a supplier and customer. It shows the invoices and credit notes sent, payments received and any outstanding balance on the account.	Remittance Advice

 Activity 6

Your organisation purchased 24 boxes of paper towels at £12.45 for each box. What is the total of the paper towels?

£ | 298.80

 Activity 7

You work for Posies and Roses Florists. A customer purchased 24 red roses at £1.75 each. The customer has requested a receipt. What is the total cost?

£ | 42.00

Activity 8

The customer who purchased the roses in Activity 7 has complained that 4 of the roses are damaged. Unfortunately, there are no more roses available so the manager has agreed to issue a credit note. How much does the customer owe after the credit note has been issued?

£ | 35.00 |

 Activity 9

Cavalier Beds
3 Brussels Road
County Road
Gloucester
GL6 6TH
Tel: 01456 698271   Fax: 01456 698272

Invoice to:	Invoice no:	67895
	Date:	28/10/X6
KP Furniture Ltd 9 Paris Street COLCHESTER CF25 1XY	VAT reg no:	488 7922 26
	Delivery note no:	6785
	Account no:	KP12

Code		Quantity	VAT rate	Unit price £	Amount excl of VAT £
MAT15K	Deluxe Mattress	5	20%	98.00	490.00

Trade discount 10%	49.00
Subtotal	441.00
VAT	88.20
Total amount payable	529.20

KAPLAN PUBLISHING

Activity 10

A customer has been sent two invoices totalling £457.98 and £69.65. They have also received a credit note for goods returned to the supplier. This credit note was for a total of £58.60. During the month, the customer paid £200.00 to the supplier.

a) What is the balance outstanding on this customer's account?

£ 269.03

b) What is the name of the document which will be sent to the customer to show these transactions and the balance outstanding?

Statement of Account

Books of prime entry

Introduction

In the previous chapter you looked at the documents that are used in cash and credit transactions. These documents now need to be summarised in **books of prime entry**.

As the documents are recorded regularly, these books are also known as **day books.**

KNOWLEDGE	CONTENTS
Working within Bookkeeping 5 Understand how to process information into the books of prime entry	1 Documents used to record transactions with customers 2 Documents used to record transactions with suppliers 3 Batch control 4 Summary and further questions

1 Documents used to record transactions with customers

1.1 Overview

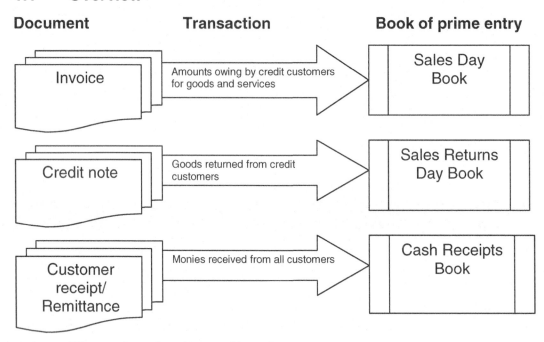

Document	Transaction	Book of prime entry
Invoice	Amounts owing by credit customers for goods and services	Sales Day Book
Credit note	Goods returned from credit customers	Sales Returns Day Book
Customer receipt/ Remittance	Monies received from all customers	Cash Receipts Book

1.2 The sales day book (SDB)

The sales day book records the individual invoices issued to credit customers. It is just a list but it will be used to perform double entry bookkeeping which you will learn about in your Level 2 accounting studies.

Example:

SALES DAY BOOK						
Date	Customer	Reference	Invoice number	Total £	VAT £	Sales £
1 July	Althams Ltd	ALT01	45787	100.00	20.00	120.00
2 July	Broadhurst plc	BRO02	45788	200.00	40.00	240.00
			TOTALS	300.00	60.00	360.00

Notes

- The reference number is the code number of the customer's account in the sales ledger.
- The invoice number is the number of the invoice issued for each sale.
- The Sales column is the total value of the goods sold as shown on the invoice after deducting trade discount including VAT.

- The amount of VAT is recorded in a separate column to show the amount owing to HMRC for these invoices.
- The Total column shows the total amount due from customers.

🔆 Example

An invoice to customer A is made up as follows:

	£
Sale of 50 units at £2 per unit	100.00
Less: 20% trade discount	(20.00)
	80.00
VAT (£80 × 20%)	16.00
Total invoice value	96.00

An invoice to customer B is made up as follows:

	£
Sale of 75 units at £2 per unit	150.00
Less: 10% trade discount	(15.00)
	135.00
VAT (£135.00 × 20%)	27.00
Total invoice value	162.00

The sales day book would therefore look as follows for the example above:

Date	Customer	Reference	Invoice number	Total £	VAT £	Sales £
	A			96.00	16.00	80.00
	B			162.00	27.00	135.00
			TOTALS	258.00	43.00	215.00

1.3 The sales returns day book

Sales returns are usually entered in a 'sales returns day book'. This is similar to the sales day book, and the columns are used in the same way. The only difference is that instead of having a column for the invoice number, there is a column for the 'credit note number'. This is because when the goods are returned by customers a credit note is issued.

SALES RETURNS DAY BOOK

Date	Customer	Reference	Credit note number	Total £	VAT £	Sales returns £

In some businesses the level of sales returns are fairly low and therefore it is not justified to keep a separate sales returns day book. In these cases any credit notes that are issued for sales returns are recorded as negative amounts in the sales day book.

1.4 The cash book

 Definition

The Cash Book records receipts and payment made by cash, cheque, credit or debit card, or bank transfer.

One of the most important books used within a business is the cash book. There are various forms of cash book, a 'two column' and a 'three column' cash book.

A two column cash book records details of cash and bank transactions separately as shown here:

CASH BOOK

Date	Details	Bank £	Cash £	Date	Details	Bank £	Cash £
		Receipts				Payments	

Notes

- The left hand side of the cash book represents the debit side – money received.
- The right hand side of the cash book represents the credit side – money paid out.
- In practice, there is usually a column on both the debit and the credit side for the date.
- The details column describes the transactions – typically the name of the customer and supplier.

- The bank column on the debit side represents money received (by cheque or other bank payment) whereas the bank column on the credit side represents money paid (by cheque or other bank payment).

Some organisations keep separate cash books to record receipts and payments. These are known as the Cash Receipts Book and Cash Payments Book, respectively.

 Definition

Monies – A term used to describe all types of payments and receipts including cash, cheques and direct bank transfers.

1.5 The petty cash book

 Definition

Petty cash is the small amount of cash that most businesses hold in order to make small cash payments.

The petty cash book is normally set out as a large ledger account with a small receipts side and a larger analysed payments side.

A typical petty cash book is set out below.

Receipts										
Date	Narrative	Total	Date	Narrative	Voucher no	Total	Postage	Cleaning	Tea & Coffee	VAT
						£	£	£	£	£
1 Nov	Bal b/f	35.50								
1 Nov	Cheque 394	114.50	1 Nov	ASDA	58	23.50			23.50	
			2 Nov	Post Office Ltd	59	29.50	29.50			
			2 Nov	Cleaning materials	60	15.07		12.56		2.51
			3 Nov	Postage	61	16.19	16.19			

The receipts side of the petty cash book only requires one column, as the only receipt into the petty cash box is the regular payment into the petty cash box of cash drawn out of the bank account.

From the example of a typical petty cash book (above), we can see that the balance brought forward was £35.50. The petty cash has then been restored up to £150 by paying in an additional £114.50.

Payments out of the petty cash box will be for a variety of different types of expense and an analysis column is required for each type of expense in the same way as the cash payments book is analysed. The example (above) has split the expenses into postage, cleaning, tea & coffee and sundry expenses. Note that a column is also required for VAT, as if a petty cash expense includes VAT this must also be analysed out.

2 Documents used to record transactions with suppliers

2.1 Overview

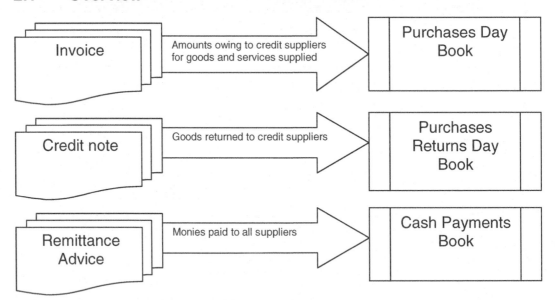

2.2 The purchases day book

As seen earlier in the chapter, credit sales are recorded in the 'sales day book'. In the case of credit purchases, we have the 'purchases day book'.

The purchases day book is simply a list of the purchases invoices that are to be processed for a given period (e.g. a week). In its simplest form, the purchases day book will comprise just the names of the suppliers and the amount of the invoices received in the week.

Purchases returns are entered in a 'purchases returns day book'. This looks similar to the purchases day book, and the columns are used in the same way. The only difference is that instead of having a column for the invoice number, there is a column for the 'credit note number'. This is because when the goods are sent back the business will receive a credit note from the supplier.

In some businesses the level of purchases returns are fairly low and therefore it is not necessary to keep a separate purchases returns day book. In these cases any credit notes that are received for purchases returns are recorded as negative amounts in the purchases day book.

 Example

You work in the accounts department of R Porte Manufacturing Ltd and one of your tasks is to sort the documents before they are entered in to the correct books of prime entry.

From the following documents, identify which book of prime entry it should be recorded in.

Document 1

R Moore Fashions

12 Dutch Corner
High Wycombe
HG4 7NQ

Invoice no: 005673
Tax point:14 July 2016

INVOICE

To: R Porte Manufacturing Ltd
   5 Ventoux Crescent, Cardiff, CA2 3HU

Product	Quantity	Price per unit	Total
		£	£
Cargo pants	5	25.00	125.00
T-shirts	10	15.00	150.00
			275.00
		VAT 20%	55.00
		Total	330.00
Payment terms: 30 days net			

Answer: You are dealing with documents for R Porte Manufacturing.

This invoice is sent **to** you at R Porte Manufacturing, so you have received it from R Moore Fashions, who must be the supplier.

Therefore, this is a supplier invoice and should be entered into the **purchases day book.**

Document 2

R Porte Manufacturing Ltd

5 Ventoux Crescent	Credit Note no: 05876
Cardiff	Tax point: 16 July 2016
CA2 3HU	

CREDIT NOTE

To: Birnies Biscuits
    Elysee Avenue, Mitcham, MA3 6ZT

Product	Quantity	Price per unit (£)	Total (£)
Packing cases	4	5.00	20.00
		VAT 20%	4.00
		Total	24.00

Payment terms: 30 days net

Answer: Remember, you are dealing with documents for R Porte Manufacturing.

This credit note is sent **to** Birnies Biscuits, so they must be the customer. Therefore, this is a customer credit note and should be entered into the **sales returns day book.**

Activity 1

Match the following documents to the relevant book of prime entry.

Invoice to customer	Cash Payments Book
Credit note from supplier	Sales Day Book
Cash received from customer	Sales Returns Day Book
Invoice from supplier	Cash Receipts Book
Credit note to customer	Purchases Day Book
Cheque paid to supplier	Purchases Returns Day Book

Activity 2

You work in the accounts department of Armistead & Co and one of your tasks is to sort the documents before they are entered in to the books of prime entry.

Armistead & Co			
Ryan's Close Lower Meltham MT4 3SQ		Invoice no: 59870 Tax point: 1 July 2016	
INVOICE			
To: Pendleton Prisms **Stuart Street, Bristol, BR1 JQ8**			
Product	Quantity	Price per unit	Total
Anti-rust bike chain	100	£3.99	£399.00
Chainset and cable kit	5	£25.00	£125.00
			£524.00
		VAT 20%	£104.80
		Total	**£628.80**
Payment terms: 15 days net			

The book of prime entry to be used is:

 Activity 3

You work in the accounts department of Birnies Biscuits and your task is to sort the documents before they are entered in to the correct books of prime entry. Which book of prime entry should be used for the following?

R Porte Manufacturing Ltd			
5 Ventoux Crescent Cardiff CA2 3HU		Credit Note no: 05876 Tax point: 16 July 2016	
CREDIT NOTE			
To: Birnies Biscuits **Elysee Avenue, Mitcham, MA3 6ZT**			
Product	Quantity	Price per unit (£)	Total (£)
Packing cases	4	5.00	20.00
		VAT 20%	4.00
		Total	24.00
Payment terms: 30 days net			

3 Batch control

3.1 Batch processing

A busy accounts office will need to record a lot of transactions and it is important that all the information is entered quickly and accurately into the correct book of prime entry.

Batch processing is a method of entering batches of similar transactions all together rather than individually. Using this method, all customer invoices, credit notes and receipts and all supplier invoices, credit notes and receipts will be sorted into separate piles before being entered into the relevant book of prime entry.

3.2 Benefits of batch processing

Batch processing will help to save time as it means that accounting staff can concentrate on one task at a time can be rather than swapping between different documents and books of prime entry. By focusing on one task at a time, it also means that fewer mistakes will be made.

Cheques and cash paid listings can be used to quickly record all the money paid out by the organisation each day. The total amount is then entered into the cash payments book.

Cheques and cash received listings can be used to record all the money received out by the organisation each day. The total amount is then entered into the cash receipts book.

4 Summary and further questions

In this chapter you learnt about the different day books used to keep of a record of the documents used in accounting transactions.

You also saw how batch control can help accounting professionals to process information efficiently and effectively.

The following practice questions will test your knowledge of this chapter.

Activity 4

Fill in the gaps below to complete the sentences. Choose from the Pick list provided.

The _____ is used to record invoices from customers.

The _____ is used to record credit notes from customers.

The _____ is used to record invoices to suppliers.

The _____ is used to record credit notes to suppliers.

The _____ is used to record monies received from customers.

The _____ is used to record monies paid to suppliers.

Pick List

Cash receipts book	Sales day book	Cash payments book
Purchases day book	Purchases returns day book	Sales returns day book

Activity 5

You have been asked to enter the invoice below into the sales day book.

P Sagan Cleaning Products	
15 Gatehead Road Maplethorpe MA1 7GZ	Invoice no: 5698 Tax point: 26 Mar 2016

INVOICE

To: G Thomas (A/C Ref TH02)
5 Holland Crescent, Chesham CA2 3HU

Product	Quantity	Price per unit	Total
Goods (Carpet – Deluxe Cleaner)	5	£50.12	£250.60
		VAT 20%	£50.12
		Total	£300.72

Payment terms: 30 days net

Complete the Sales Day Book below with the correct information.

Date	Customer	Reference	Invoice No	Total £	VAT £	Net £

Activity 6

Complete the sentence below with the correct options.

Batch processing is a method of processing financial documents [all together/individually] rather than [all together/individually].

 Activity 7

You work in the accounts department of Foe & Co and one of your tasks is to sort the documents before they are entered in to the books of prime entry.

Foe & Co			
Middlebrow		Invoice no: 598	
MI4 3SQ		Tax point: 18 July 20X6	
Credit Note			
To: Fi and Fun			
Rose Avenue, Cardiff, CT1 JQ8			
Product	Quantity	Price per unit	Total
KBM15	1	£35.99	£35.99
		VAT 20%	£7.19
		Total	**£43.18**
Payment terms: 15 days net			

Which daybook should this document be entered in?

Activity 8

You work in the accounts department of Diamond Ltd and one of your tasks is to sort the documents before they are entered in to the books of prime entry.

King & Co			
Highbrow		Invoice no: 2867	
HI4 3SQ		Tax point: 18 June 20X6	
Invoice			
To: Diamond Ltd			
Platt Avenue, Delph, OL1 JQ8			
Product	*Quantity*	*Price per unit*	*Total*
Item 5	10	£35.50	£355.00
		VAT 20%	£71.00
		Total	£426.00
Payment terms: 15 days net			

Which daybook should this document be entered in?

Activity 9

You work in the accounts department of Diamond Ltd and you have been asked to send a cheque to a supplier for payment of goods.

Which daybook should the amount be listed in?

Activity 10

Complete the sentences below by choosing the correct options:

Cheques and cash paid into the organisation can be listed on a **cheques and cash paid/cheques and cash received** listing before entering into the **cash payments book/cash receipts book.**

This is an example of **batch processing/invoice processing** and means that **more/fewer** mistakes will be made.

Answers to chapter activities

Activity 1

Invoice to customer	=	Sales Day Book
Credit note from supplier	=	Purchase Returns Day Book
Cash received from customer	=	Cash Receipts Book
Invoice from supplier	=	Purchases Day Book
Credit note to customer	=	Sales Returns Day Book
Cheque paid to supplier	=	Cash Payments Book

Activity 2

You are dealing with documents for Armistead & Co. This invoice is **to** Pendleton Prisms, so they must be the customer.

Therefore, this is a customer invoice and should be entered into the **sales day book.**

Activity 3

You are dealing with documents for Birnies Biscuits. This credit note is **from** R Porte Manufacturing, so they must be the supplier.

Therefore, this is a supplier credit note and should be entered in the **purchase returns day book.**

Activity 4

The **Sales day book** is used to record invoices from customers.

The **Sales returns day book** is used to record credit notes from customers.

The **Purchases day book** is used to record invoices to suppliers.

The **Purchases returns day book** is used to record credit notes to suppliers.

The **Cash receipts book** is used to record monies received from customers.

The **Cash payments book** is used to record monies paid to suppliers.

 Activity 5

Date	Customer	Reference	Invoice No	Total £	VAT £	Net £
26 Mar 2016	G Thomas	TH02	5698	300.72	50.12	250.60

 Activity 6

Batch processing is a method of processing financial documents [**all together**] rather than [**individually**].

 Activity 7

You are dealing with documents for Foe & Co. This credit note is **to** Fi and Fun, so they must be the customer.

Therefore, this is a credit note sent to a customer and should be entered into the **sales returns day book.**

 Activity 8

You are dealing with documents for Diamond Ltd. This invoice is sent from King and Co who must be the supplier of the goods.

Therefore, this is an invoice received from a supplier and should be entered into the **purchases day book.**

Activity 9

You work in the accounts department of Diamond Ltd and you have been asked to send a cheque to a supplier for payment of goods. Therefore this is a payment and should be listed in the **cash payments book.**

 Activity 10

Cheques and cash paid into the organisation can be listed on a **cheques and cash received listing** before entering into the **cash receipts book.**

This is an example of **batch processing** and means that **fewer** mistakes will be made.

Cheques and paying-in slips

Introduction

There are many different ways a business can make and receive payments. A lot of businesses make electronic payments, however a lot of customers still pay in cash or by writing a cheque. When physical payments are received by an organisation, the monies will need to be paid into the business's bank account.

This chapter explains how to complete the documents used in banking transactions.

KNOWLEDGE	CONTENTS
This is essential background knowledge for any bookkeeper although will not be directly assessed.	1 Paying-in slips 2 Cheques 3 Summary and further questions

1 Paying-in slips

1.1 Paying-in slips

All business organisations are provided with a paying-in book by the bank. Each paying-in book contains paying-in slips. When money is paid into the bank it is accompanied by one of the completed paying-in slips.

If your job is to pay money into the bank, you will need to complete and sign the bank paying-in slip taken from the paying-in book. The paying-in slip is then given to the bank cashier who will check it against the monies being paid in to the bank.

1.2 Example of a paying-in slip

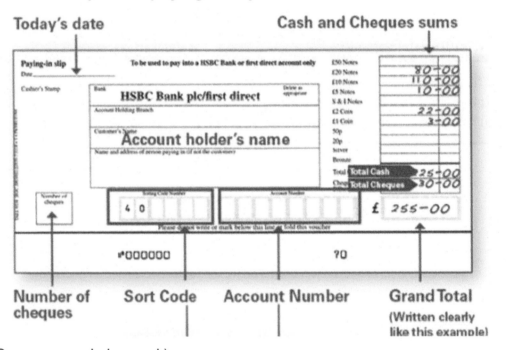

(Source: www.hsbc.co.uk)

1.3 Paying-in requirements and records

You only need to enter the number of cheques being paid in and the total amount on the front of the paying in slip. On the back of the paying in slip you should write a list of the cheques being paid in.

The paying-in stub is the part of the paying-in slip which stays in the paying-in book and is a record for the organisation of the amounts paid into the bank.

Activity 1

Today's date is 19 July 2015.

You have been asked to complete a bank paying-in slip for the money received today, which is as follows:

Notes	Coins	Cheques
3 x £20 notes	25 x £1 coins	Thomas £1,500.00
15 x £10 notes	8 x 50p coins	Friebe £ 750.00
20 x £5 notes	20 x 10p coins	

Complete the paying-in slip below:

Date:	Main Bank plc	£50 notes	
	Cartown	£20 notes	
		£10 notes	
	Account	£5 notes	
	ABC Ltd	£2 coin	
		£1 coin	
No of cheques	Paid in by	Other coin	
	AAT Student	Total cash	
	Sort Code Account No	Cheques	
	10-11-44 12879065	Total £	

 Activity 2

Why is it important that the paying-in slip is dated and signed?

2 Cheques

2.1 The use of cheques

When a person (or organisation) writes a cheque they are instructing their bank to transfer a specified amount of money from their bank account to the bank account of the recipient of the cheque – the payee.

If the cheque hasn't been completed correctly the bank may return it to the payee. The payee will then have to ask for a replacement cheque from the organisation.

As this causes delays in the payment process, it is important that the cheque is completed correctly in the first place.

2.2 Cheque requirements

For a cheque to be valid it should include:

- **Payee name** The payee is the person or organisation to whom the cheque is written. The payee's name should exactly match the name on their bank account.

- **Date** The date that the cheque is written must include the day, month and the year. A cheque that is more than 6 months old is invalid and the bank will not accept the cheque.

- **Words** The pounds part of the amount being paid must be written in words but the pence part can be written in numbers. If the amount is a whole number of pounds then you should write 'ONLY' after the amount to prevent someone changing the figure.

- **Numbers** The amount being paid should be written in numbers in the box on the right hand side of the cheque. The amount in numbers should exactly match the amount written in words.

- **Signature** The cheque should be signed by an authorised signatory of the organisation.

 Definition

Signatories – a person or persons who are authorised to sign cheques on behalf of an organisation.

Example

ABC Bank PLC	Date: 30th January 20X5
Payee: *Mr John Smith*	
	£350.00
Three hundred and fifty pounds only	MISS ANNE JONES

CHEQUE NO	SORT CODE	ACCOUNT NO
04312	25-22-78	30087251

Activity 3

Today's date is 29th July 2015 and you have been given the following cheques to complete. Fill in the gaps using the correct numbers, words and/or date.

Cheque A

ABC Bank PLC	Date: 29th July, 2015
Payee: *Mr G Thomas*	
Five hundred pounds ONLY	on behalf of TDF Ltd

CHEQUE NO	SORT CODE	ACCOUNT NO
04312	25-22-78	30087251

Cheque B

ABC Bank PLC	Date: 29th July, 2015
Payee: *Armistead & Co*	
	250.50
	on behalf of TDF Ltd

CHEQUE NO	SORT CODE	ACCOUNT NO
04312	25-22-78	30087251

Cheque C

ABC Bank PLC	Date:
Payee: *Mr P Sagan*	
	25.20
Twenty five pounds and 20p only	on behalf of TDF Ltd

CHEQUE NO	SORT CODE	ACCOUNT NO
04312	25-22-78	30087251

3   Summary and further questions

In this chapter, you were introduced to two documents used in banking procedures.

The paying-in slip should be completed correctly and should match the monies being paid into the bank.

For cheques to be valid they need to be made out to the correct payee, the words and numbers need to match exactly, and the cheques need to be signed by an authorised person.

The following questions will test your knowledge of this chapter:

Activity 4

Write the following words as numbers to two decimal places:

Five hundred and fifty pounds	
Twenty two pounds and thirty four pence	
Five hundred pounds and five pence	
One thousand, two hundred and twenty pounds	

Activity 5

Write the following amounts in words:

£20.50	
£678.90	
£1400.40	
£89.00	

Activity 6

Cheques can be signed by anyone in an organisation. True or False?

KAPLAN PUBLISHING

Activity 7

Match the definitions with the correct words used in banking

A person who is authorised to sign documents on behalf of an organisation	payee
The person or organisation to whom the cheque is written	stub
A written instruction to transfer a specified sum of money from one bank account to another.	monies
The part of a cheque or paying-in slip kept as a record of the transaction	signatory
The term used to describe different forms of payments and receipts including cash, cheques and direct bank transfers.	cheque

 Activity 8

As long as a cheque has been completed correctly it is valid for ever.

True or False?

Answers to chapter activities

Activity 1

Date:	Main Bank plc	£50 notes	
	Cartown	£20 notes	60.00
		£10 notes	150.00
	Account	£5 notes	100.00
	ABC Ltd	£2 coin	
		£1 coin	25.00
No of cheques	Paid in by	Other coin	6.00
	AAT Student	Total cash	341.00
	Sort Code Account No	Cheques	2250.00
	10-11-44 12879065	Total £	2591.00

Activity 2

The paying-in slip must be dated and signed so that the bank cashier can contact the person who paid in the money in to the bank, in case there are any queries.

Activity 3

Cheque A - The amount in numbers should be £500.00

ABC Bank PLC	Date: 29th July, 2015
Payee: *Mr G Thomas*	
	500.00
Five hundred pounds ONLY	on behalf of TDF Ltd
CHEQUE NO SORT CODE ACCOUNT NO	
04312 25-22-78 30087251	

Cheque B - The amount in words should be 'Two hundred and fifty pounds and 50p'

ABC Bank PLC	Date: 29th July, 2015

ABC Bank PLC   Date: 29th July, 2015

Payee: *Armistead & Co*

250.50

Two hundred and fifty pounds and 50p   on behalf of TDF Ltd

CHEQUE NO	SORT CODE	ACCOUNT NO
04312	25-22-78	30087251

Cheque C - The date should contain the day, the month and the year. For example: 29th July 2015, 29 Jul 15, or 29/07/15 are all correct.

ABC Bank PLC   Date: ***29th July, 2015***

Payee: *Mr P Sagan*

25.20

Twenty five pounds and 20p only   on behalf of TDF Ltd

CHEQUE NO	SORT CODE	ACCOUNT NO
04312	25-22-78	30087251

Activity 4

Five hundred and fifty pounds	£550.00
Twenty two pounds and thirty four pence	£22.34
Five hundred pounds and five pence	£500.05
One thousand, two hundred and twenty pounds	£1220.00

Activity 5

£20.50	Twenty pounds and fifty pence
£678.90	Six hundred and seventy eight pounds and ninety pence
£1400.40	One thousand four hundred pounds and forty pence
£89.00	Eighty nine pounds

Activity 6

The statement is false. Cheques can only be signed by authorised signatories.

 Activity 7

Match the definitions with the correct words used in banking

A person who are authorised to sign documents on behalf of an organisation

The person or organisation to whom the cheque is written

A written instruction to transfer a specified sum of money from one bank account to another.

The part of a cheque or paying-in slip kept as a record of the transaction

The term used to describe different forms of payments and receipts including cash, cheques and direct bank transfers.

payee

stub

monies

signatory

cheque

 Activity 8

As long as a cheque has been completed correctly it is valid for ever.

This statement is **false.** Banks will refuse to accept cheques which are banked 6 months after the date written on the cheque.

Bookkeeping basics

Introduction

This chapter covers the basics of bookkeeping within an organisation, including:

- the role and career progression of a bookkeeper
- the need for keeping information secure within an organisation
- single entry bookkeeping, and when it might be used
- the all-important double entry bookkeeping, and what it represents
- balancing the ledger accounts and compiling the balances to produce
- the Trial Balance

KNOWLEDGE
Introduction to Bookkeeping
1 Understand the job role and career path for a bookkeeper
2 Understand different types of business organisation
3.1 Identify the difference between a bookkeeper and an accountant
Working within bookkeeping
1 Understand single entry bookkeeping
3 Understand what is meant by both cash and credit transactions
6 Understand responsibilities when working in a bookkeeping environment
Bookkeeping and accounts
2 Be able to record cash and credit transactions in books of original entry
5 Be able to extract a trial balance from ledger accounting

CONTENTS

1 Single and double entry bookkeeping
2 Debit and credit entries
3 Balancing a ledger account
4 The trial balance
5 Summary

1 Single and double entry bookkeeping

1.1 Single entry bookkeeping

Many small businesses, particularly sole traders, are cash based, or do not have many transactions to record. For this reason the owner will often only use a cash book or spreadsheet to record the income and expenditure of the business.

	A	B
1	Cstd	Sstd
2	0.000	0.00
3	0.100	12.36
4	0.200	24.83
5	0.300	35.91
6	0.400	48.79
7	0.500	60.42

The spreadsheet will often have columns analysed by type. The cash book may not.

It is quicker and easier for the owner to record the transactions this way, but the records are incomplete, and will have to be reconstructed in order to work out the taxable profit.

1.2 Double entry bookkeeping

Most organisations use double entry bookkeeping to record the financial transactions of the business.

Due to the large volume of transactions (and therefore the increased chance of error), the process is divided into three parts.

a) The transactions are first recorded in a book of prime (first) entry, also referred to as "day books".
b) The second part is the general ledger itself where the double entry takes place
c) The third part is, depending on the transaction, the sales ledger or purchase ledger which contains the individual customer and supplier accounts. (These ledgers are also known as the subsidiary (sales/purchase) ledger.

The books of prime entry have already been addressed earlier in this book. Next in the process is the double entry.

Double entry bookkeeping is based upon the principle of the dual effect.

1.3 The dual effect principle

This states that every transaction has two financial effects.

(a) If, for example, you spend £2,000 on a car and pay for it by a cheque, you will have £2,000 less money in the bank, but you will also have acquired an asset worth £2,000.

This can be viewed as:

Gained: a £2,000 car

Lost: £2,000 in cash.

The accounting terms used for this transaction are: **debit** and **credit**.

In the above example, the **debit** is the gain of a car, the **credit** is the loss of the money.

Using the accounting terminology, look at the example below:

(b) If you buy from a supplier £100 of goods and send him a cheque for that amount, you will gain £100 worth of goods, but you will have £100 less money in the bank.

Debit   £100 of goods

Credit £100 from the bank account

At first it can seem difficult, but break the transaction into two parts.

Ask:

* What did I get?
* What did I lose?

Example 1

	Debit (gain)	Credit (loss)
a) Purchases goods for resale, paid £800.	Purchases	Bank
b) Pays rent for use of office of £500.	Rent	Bank
c) Buys a van, cost £2,000.	Van	Bank
d) Sells some of the goods for £600.	Bank	Sales
e) Sells some more of the goods for £700.	Bank	Sales
f) Purchases goods for resale for £1,000.	Purchases	Bank
g) Buys stationery for £200.	Stationery	Bank

Explanation for the above example follows:

a) Gains goods to sell on, loses £800 of money from bank account

b) Gains office space, but loses £500 of money from bank account

c) Gains a van, but loses £2,000 of money from bank account

d) Gains £600, which is paid into bank account, but loses some of the goods previously bought

e) Gains some money, £700, but more goods go out the door

f) Gains some more goods to sell on, but spends (loses) £1,000 from bank account

g) Gains some stationery to write on, but loses £200 from bank account

---

 Activity 1

Bill makes the following cash transactions:

State which account will be debited and which will be credited.

	Debit (gain)	Credit (loss)
Purchases goods for resale for £700.		
Customer entertainment £300 for product launch.		
Purchases three computers for £3,000.		
Sells goods for £1,500.		
Purchases goods for resale for £1,200.		
Pays telephone bill of £600.		
Receives telephone bill rebate of £200.		
Purchases stationery for £157.		

---

2 Debit and credit entries

2.1 Debit and credit entries

We need to appreciate the effect a debit or a credit entry will have.

Ledger account	
A **debit entry** represents:	A **credit entry** represents:
• An increase in the value of an asset;	• A decrease in the value of an asset;
• A decrease in the value of a liability; or	• An increase in the value of a liability; or
• An increase to an item of expenditure	• An increase to an item of income (revenue)
• A decrease to an item of income	• A decrease to an item of expense.

2.2 DEAD CLIC

The mnemonic DEAD CLIC may help to remind you of which side the account balances should be.

Notice that some transactions are for cash (immediate payment) and some are credit transactions (payment will be made at a later date).

DEAD   **CLIC**

Debits: **Credits:**

Expenses   Liabilities

Assets   Income

Drawings   Capital

 Example 2

Notice that some transactions are for cash (immediate) and some for credit. The ones that are credit transactions name the customer or supplier, so their name is used as the account to be debited or credited. Again, think carefully about what is going on.

		DR	CR
July 1	Started business with £3,000 cash	Cash	Capital*
July 3	Bought goods for cash £850	Purchases	Cash
July 7	Bought goods on credit £1,160 from E Morgan	Purchases	E Morgan
July 10	Sold goods for cash £420	Cash	Sales
July 14	Returned goods to E Morgan £280	E Morgan	Purchase Returns
July 18	Bought goods on credit £980 from A Moses	Purchases	A Moses
July 21	Returned goods to A Moses £190	A Moses	Purchase Returns
July 24	Sold goods to A Knight £550 on credit	A Knight	Sales
July 25	Paid E Morgan's account by cash £880	E Morgan	Cash
July 31	A Knight paid us his account in cash £550	Cash	A Knight

*Capital is the name for the money the owner 'lends' to the business, that is why Capital is a credit.

In the example above the individual customer and supplier names are used. All the customers make up the **Sales ledger** or **Debtors** (see chapter 2), and all the suppliers make up the **Purchase ledger** or **Creditors.**

In the above example the Sales ledger and Purchase ledger are made up as follows:

Sales ledger   **Purchase ledger**

A Knight   E Morgan

                                                                        A Moses

A business needs to know not only how much an individual customer owes, but also how much is due to the organisation from all the customers added together, so to work out how much in all is owed to the business the customer account balances are added together to get the total amount due.

The total of the customer balances is known as the **Sales ledger control account**, and it is this total figure that goes into the trial balance. The same applies to the purchase ledger. The **Purchase ledger control account** is the total of the money due to all the suppliers.

Let's add some more customers, and some balances (the total amount owed to the organisation by the customers).

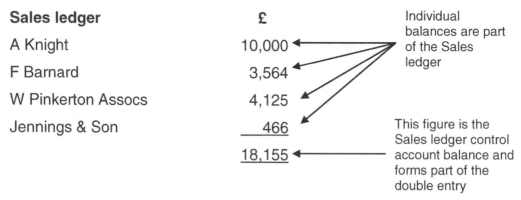

Sales ledger	£	
A Knight	10,000	Individual balances are part of the Sales ledger
F Barnard	3,564	
W Pinkerton Assocs	4,125	
Jennings & Son	466	
	18,155	This figure is the Sales ledger control account balance and forms part of the double entry

The Sales ledger is made up of the individual customer balances, but the **Sales ledger control account** is the grand total, and it's that overall figure that is part of the double entry and forms part of the Trial Balance (see later in the chapter).

The **Purchase ledger** and **Purchase ledger control account** work in the same way.

KAPLAN PUBLISHING

Activity 2

Now you have a go.

Identify the two accounts needed for each transaction and whether they are a debit or a credit:

		DR	CR
Aug 4	Bought goods on credit £780 from S Holmes		
Aug 5	Bought a motor van by cheque £5,000		
Aug 7	Bought goods for cash £550		
Aug 10	Sold goods on credit £980 to D Moore		
Aug 12	Returned goods to S Holmes £180		
Aug 19	Sold goods for cash £280		
Aug 22	Bought fixtures on credit from Kingston Equipment Co £1,500		
Aug 24	D Watson lent us £1,000 paying us the money by cheque		
Aug 29	We paid S Holmes his account by cheque £600		
Aug 31	We paid Kingston Equipment Co by cheque £1,500		

So far you:

• Understand single entry bookkeeping and why some organisations use it.

• Understand the dual effect of double entry bookkeeping.

• Identified the two 'sides' of a transaction (gain something, lose something).

• Identified the accounts in which to place each side of the transaction.

The next step is to apply this knowledge by placing the entries into the correct accounts.

Example

We will now put debits and credits into the accounts using Example 1:

		Debit	Credit
a)	Purchases goods for resale, paid £800.	Purchases	Bank
b)	Pays rent for use of office of £500.	Rent	Bank
c)	Buys a van, cost £2,000.	Van	Bank
d)	Sells some of the goods for £600.	Bank	Sales
e)	Sells some more of the goods for £700.	Bank	Sales
f)	Purchases goods for resale for £1,000.	Purchases	Bank
g)	Buys stationery for £200.	Stationery	Bank

Debit   **Purchases account**   **Credit**

Date	Details	£	Date	Details	£
(a)	Bank	800			
(f)	Bank	1,000			

Debit   **Bank account**   **Credit**

Date	Details	£	Date	Details	£
(d)	Sales	600	(a)	Purchases	800
(e)	Sales	700	(b)	Rent	500
			(c)	Van	2,000
			(f)	Purchases	1,000
			(g)	Stationery	200

Debit   **Rent account**   **Credit**

Date	Details	£	Date	Details	£
(b)	Bank	500			

Debit   **Van account**   **Credit**

Date	Details	£	Date	Details	£
(c)	Bank	2,000			

Debit   **Sales account**   **Credit**

Date	Details	£	Date	Details	£
			(d)	Bank	600
			(e)	Sales	700

Debit   **Stationery account**   **Credit**

Date	Details	£	Date	Details	£
(g)	Bank	200			

Note:

Notice how when you enter the amount into the account, e.g. Purchases, £800, in the details you have to write where the other half of the transaction is, Bank. Failure to do so will mean that you could get in a muddle and not be able to identify where the other side of the transaction was put, particularly with the longer exercises.

Activity 3

Using the technique from the previous example above, enter the debits and credits into the accounts below.

		DR	CR
July 1	Started business with £3,000 cash	Cash	Capital*
July 3	Bought goods for cash £850	Purchases	Cash
July 7	Bought goods on credit £1,160 from E Morgan	Purchases	E Morgan
July 10	Sold goods for cash £420	Cash	Sales
July 14	Returned goods to E Morgan £280	E Morgan	Purchase Returns
July 18	Bought goods on credit £980 from A Moses	Purchases	A Moses
July 21	Returned goods to A Moses £190	A Moses	Purchase Returns
July 24	Sold goods to A Knight £550 on credit	A Knight	Sales
July 25	Paid E Morgan's account by cash £880	E Morgan	Cash
July 31	A Knight paid us his account in cash £550	Cash	A Knight

Debit   **Capital account**   **Credit**

Date	Details	£	Date	Details	£

Debit   **Purchases account**   **Credit**

Date	Details	£	Date	Details	£

Debit			Cash account		Credit
Date	Details	£	Date	Details	£

Debit			E Morgan (Supplier) account		Credit
Date	Details	£	Date	Details	£

Debit			Sales account		Credit
Date	Details	£	Date	Details	£

Debit			Purchase returns account		Credit
Date	Details	£	Date	Details	£

Debit			A Moses (supplier) account		Credit
Date	Details	£	Date	Details	£

Debit			A Knight (customer) account		Credit
Date	Details	£	Date	Details	£

Please keep your answers for this activity as they will be used later.

3 Balancing a ledger account

3.1 Procedure for balancing a ledger account

An organisation needs to know how much it has spent, and on what. In order to gain that information a balance on each account needs to be calculated:

This is done as follows:

Step 1   Total both the debit and the credit side of the ledger account and make a note of each total.

Step 2   Insert the higher of the two totals as the total on both sides of the ledger account leaving a line beneath the final entry on each side of the account.

Step 3   On the side with the smaller total insert the figure needed to make this column add up to the total. Call this figure the balance carried down (or 'Bal c/d' as an abbreviation).

Step 4   On the opposite side of the ledger account, below the total insert this same figure and call it the balance brought down (or 'Bal b/d' as an abbreviation).

An example of the method is below.

Example

The bank account of a business has the following entries:

Bank

	£		£
Capital	1,000	Purchases	200
Sales	300	Drawings	100
Sales	400	Rent	400
Capital	500	Stationery	300
Sales	800	Purchases	400

Calculate the balance on the account and bring the balance down as a single amount.

Step 1   Total both sides of the account and make a note of the totals. (Note that these totals that are asterisked below would not normally be written into the ledger account itself.)

Bank

	£		£
Capital	1,000	Purchases	200
Sales	300	Drawings	100
Sales	400	Rent	400
Capital	500	Stationery	300
Sales	800	Purchases	400
Sub-total debits*	3,000	Sub-total credits*	1,400

Step 2 Insert the higher total as the total of both sides.

Bank

	£		£
Capital	1,000	Purchases	200
Sales	300	Drawings	100
Sales	400	Rent	400
Capital	500	Stationery	300
Sales	800	Purchases	400
Sub-total debits*	3,000	Sub-total credits*	1,400
Total	3,000	Total	3,000

Step 3 Insert a balancing figure on the side of the account with the lower sub-total. This is referred to as the 'balance carried down' or 'bal c/d' for short.

Bank

	£		£
Capital	1,000	Purchases	200
Sales	300	Drawings	100
Sales	400	Rent	400
Capital	500	Stationery	300
Sales	800	Purchases	400
Sub-total debits*	3,000	Sub-total credits*	1,400
		Bal c/d	1,600
Total	3,000	Total	3,000

Step 4   Insert the balance carried down figure beneath the total on the other side of the account. This is referred to as 'bal b/d' for short.

Bank

	£		£
Capital	1,000	Purchases	200
Sales	300	Drawings	100
Sales	400	Rent	400
Capital	500	Stationery	300
Sales	800	Purchases	400
*Sub-total debits**	*3,000*	*Sub-total credits**	*1,400*
		Bal c/d	1,600
Total	3,000	Total	3,000
Bal b/d	1,600		

The closing balance carried down at the end of the period is also the opening balance brought down at the start of the next period. This opening balance remains in the account as the starting position and any further transactions are then added into the account. In this case the balance brought down is a debit balance as there is money in the bank account making it an asset.

💡 Example

Consider the ledger accounts below and balance them.

The double entry transactions have been numbered to help identify the two sides.

Bank

Date			£	Date			£
1 Jan	Capital	(1)	20,000	1 Jan	Van	(2)	500
5 Jan	Sales	(6)	2,000		Purchases	(3)	1,000
					Drawings	(4)	50
				5 Jan	Purchases	(5)	500
				15 Jan	Rent	(7)	200

Capital

Date			£	Date			£
				1 Jan	Bank	(1)	20,000

Van

Date			£	Date	£
1 Jan	Bank	(2)	500		

Purchases

Date			£	Date	£
1 Jan	Bank	(3)	1,000		
5 Jan	Bank	(5)	500		

Drawings

Date			£	Date	£
1 Jan	Bank	(4)	50		

Sales

Date	£	Date			£
		5 Jan	Bank	(6)	2,000

Rent

Date			£	Date	£
15 Jan	Bank	(7)	200		

Solution

a)   The bank account

Bank

Date		£	Date		£
1 Jan	Capital	20,000	1 Jan	Van	500
5 Jan	Sales	2,000		Purchases	1,000
				Drawings	50
			5 Jan	Purchases	500
			15 Jan	Rent	200

Step 1   Total both the debit and the credit side of the ledger account and make a note of each total – debit side £22,000, credit side £2,250.

Step 2   Insert the higher of the two totals, £22,000, as the total on both sides of the ledger account leaving a line beneath the final entry on each side of the account.

Bank

Date		£	Date		£
1 Jan	Capital	20,000	1 Jan	Van	500
5 Jan	Sales	2,000		Purchases	1,000
				Drawings	50
			5 Jan	Purchases	500
			15 Jan	Rent	200
		22,000			22,000

Step 3   On the side with the smaller total insert the figure needed to

Step 4 make this column add up to the total. Call this figure the balance carried down (or Bal c/d as an abbreviation).

Step 4 On the opposite side of the ledger account, below the total insert this same figure and call it the balance brought down (or Bal b/d as an abbreviation).

Bank

Date		£	Date		£
1 Jan	Capital	20,000	1 Jan	Van	500
5 Jan	Sales	2,000		Purchases	1,000
				Drawings	50
			5 Jan	Purchases	500
			15 Jan	Rent	200
			31 Jan	Balance c/d	19,750
		22,000			22,000
1 Feb	Balance b/d	19,750			

f) Sales

Sales

Date		£	Date		£
			5 Jan	Bank	2,000

There is no need to balance the account as there is only one entry – a £2,000 credit balance representing income.

g) Rent

Rent

Date		£	Date		£
15 Jan	Bank	200			

As there is only one entry there is no need to balance the account. This is a debit balance indicating that there has been an expense of £200 of rent incurred during the month.

Activity 4

Given below is a bank account ledger account for the month of March. You are required to "balance off" the ledger account.

Bank

Date		£	Date		£
1 Mar	Capital	12,000	3 Mar	Purchases	3,000
7 Mar	Sales	5,000	15 Mar	Non-current asset	2,400
19 Mar	Sales	2,000	20 Mar	Purchases	5,300
22 Mar	Sales	3,000	24 Mar	Rent	1,000
			28 Mar	Drawings	2,000

4 The trial balance

4.1 List of balances

The trial balance is a list showing the balances brought down on each ledger account. An example of a simple trial balance is given below:

	Debit £	Credit £
Sales		5,000
Opening inventory	100	
Purchases	3,000	
Rent	200	
Car	3,000	
SLCAs	100	
PLCA		1,400
	6,400	6,400

The trial balance is produced immediately after the double entry has been completed and the account balances calculated. If the double entry has been done correctly, the total of the debits will equal the total of the credits.

4.2 Reasons for extracting a trial balance

Drafting a trial balance is a way of ensuring that double entries have been correctly completed. It is possible to detect errors with a trial balance, but this is not relevant to the Level 1 Assessment.

Example

The following are the balances on the accounts of Ernest at 31 December 20X8. Prepare Ernest's trial balance as at 31 December 20X8.

	£
Sales	47,140
Purchases	26,500
SLCAs	7,640
PLCA	4,320
General expenses	9,430
Loan	5,000
Plant and machinery at cost	7,300
Motor van at cost	2,650
Drawings	7,500
Rent and rates	6,450
Insurance	1,560
Bank overdraft	2,570
Capital	10,000

Solution

Step 1   Set up a blank trial balance

Step 2   Work down the list of balances one by one using what you have learned so far about debits and credits. Assets and expenses are debit balances and liabilities, income and capital are credit balances.

Trial balance at 31 December 20X8

	Dr £	Cr £
Sales		47,140
Purchases	26,500	
SLCAs	7,640	
PLCA		4,320
General expenses	9,430	
Loan		5,000
Plant and machinery at cost	7,300	
Motor van at cost	2,650	
Drawings	7,500	
Rent and rates	6,450	
Insurance	1,560	
Bank overdraft		2,570
Capital		10,000
	69,030	69,030

Take care with drawings. These are a reduction of the capital owed back to the owner therefore as a reduction of a liability they must be a debit balance.

The bank overdraft is an amount owed to the bank therefore it must be a credit balance.

 Activity 5

Refer to your answers in Activity 3. Balance off the accounts, and then draw up a Trial Balance from those balances.

If you have lost your answers, then have another go at Activity 7 and see how much you have improved!

5 Summary

In this chapter we have studied cash and credit transactions. It is important to always start with the bank account and remember that cash received is a debit in the bank account and cash paid out is a credit in the bank account. If you get that right then the rest really does fall into place.

You should also be aware of the definitions of assets, expenses and income and the normal entries you would make in the accounts for these.

Balancing an account is a very important technique which you must be able to master. You must understand how to bring the balance down onto the correct side and what that balance represents.

Answers to chapter activities

Activity 1

	Debit (gain)	Credit (loss)
Purchases goods for resale for £700.	Purchases	Bank
Customer entertainment £300 for product launch.	Entertainment	Bank
Purchases three computers for £3,000.	Computers	Bank
Sells goods for £1,500.	Bank	Sales
Purchases goods for resale for £1,200.	Purchases	Bank
Pays telephone bill of £600.	Telephone	Bank
Receives telephone bill rebate of £200.	Bank	Telephone
Purchases stationery for £157.	Stationery	Bank

Activity 2

		DR	CR
Aug 4	Bought goods on credit £780 from S Holmes	Purchases	S Holmes
Aug 5	Bought a motor van by cheque £5,000	Van	Bank
Aug 7	Bought goods for cash £550	Purchases	Cash
Aug 10	Sold goods on credit £980 to D Moore	D Moore	Sales
Aug 12	Returned goods to S Holmes £180	S Holmes	Purchase Returns
Aug 19	Sold goods for cash £280	Cash	Sales
Aug 22	Bought fixtures on credit from Kingston Equipment Co £1,500	Fixtures	Kingston Equipment
Aug 24	D Watson lent us £1,000 paying us the money by cheque	Bank	D Watson - Loan
Aug 29	We paid S Holmes his account by cheque £600	S Holmes	Bank
Aug 31	We paid Kingston Equipment Co by cheque £1,500	Kingston Equipment	Bank

Activity 3

Debit   **Capital account**   **Credit**

Date	Details	£	Date	Details	£
			July 1	Cash	3,000

Debit   **Purchases account**   **Credit**

Date	Details	£	Date	Details	£
July 3	Cash	850			
July 7	E Morgan	1,160			
July 18	A Moses	980			

Debit   **Cash account**   **Credit**

Date	Details	£	Date	Details	£
July 1	Capital	3,000	July 3	Purchases	850
July 10	Sales	420	July 25	E Morgan	880
July 31	A Knight	550			

Debit   **E Morgan (Supplier) account**   **Credit**

Date	Details	£	Date	Details	£
July 14	Purchases returns	280	July 7	Cash	1,160
July 25	Cash	880			

Debit   **Sales account**   **Credit**

Date	Details	£	Date	Details	£
			July 10	Cash	420
			July 24	A Knight	550

Debit   **Purchase returns account**   **Credit**

Date	Details	£	Date	Details	£
			July 14	E Morgan	280
			July 21	A Moses	190

Debit   **A Moses (supplier) account**   **Credit**

Date	Details	£	Date	Details	£
July 21	Purchase returns	190	July 18	Purchases	980

Debit   **A Knight (customer) account**   **Credit**

Date	Details	£	Date	Details	£
July 24	Sales	550	July 31	Cash	550

KAPLAN PUBLISHING

Activity 4

Bank

Date		£	Date		£
1 Mar	Capital	12,000	3 Mar	Purchases	3,000
7 Mar	Sales	5,000	15 Mar	Non-current asset	2,400
19 Mar	Sales	2,000	20 Mar	Purchases	5,300
22 Mar	Sales	3,000	24 Mar	Rent	1,000
			28 Mar	Drawings	2,000
			31 Mar	Balance c/d	8,300
		22,000			22,000
1 Apr	Balance b/d	8,300			

Activity 5

Trial balance at 31 August 20X9

	Dr £	Cr £
Capital		3,000
Purchases	2,990	
Cash	2,240	
Purchase ledger control account		790
Sales		970
Purchase returns		470
	5,230	5,230

From the day books to the general ledger

7

Introduction

The general ledger is the place where the double entry takes place in the appropriate ledger accounts.

KNOWLEDGE
Bookkeeping and accounts
2 Be able to record cash and credit transactions in books of original entry

CONTENTS

1 The general ledger

1.1 The general ledger

The general ledger contains all the accounts you have become familiar with so far, for example:

- Capital
- Drawings
- Van
- Rent
- Electricity
- Purchases
- Bank

Each account contains a record of transactions over a given period. At the end of each period, usually each month, the accounts are balanced off to give a total of the transactions in each account. The account balances are then transferred to a trial balance.

Two of these typical accounts are the Customer and Supplier accounts but now we will call these the **sales ledger control account** and the **purchases ledger control account**.

The sales ledger control account shows the total amount outstanding from customers and the purchases ledger control account shows the total amount owing to suppliers.

Note: the AAT refers to this ledger as the general ledger. In some businesses it is referred to as the 'main ledger' or the 'nominal ledger'. Be prepared to use any one of these terms when you are at work.

1.2 The sales ledger

Not only is it important to track how much money the customers in total owe the business, we also have to keep track of how much each individual customer owes the organisation. How much was the customer invoiced? How much has the customer paid? How much does the customer owe?

A separate account for each customer is held in a separate subsidiary sales ledger. This ledger is not part of the general ledger and is not part of the double entry system. Transactions with credit customers are recorded in both the sales ledger control account in the general ledger and the customers' individual account in the subsidiary sales ledger.

The sales ledger contains a separate ledger account for each individual customer. Every individual invoice and cash receipt is posted to an individual's account in the sales ledger.

1.3 The purchases ledger

As we require information about individual customers, the same applies to individual suppliers. How much have we been invoiced? What have we paid? How much do we owe?

A separate account for each supplier is held in a separate subsidiary purchases ledger. Transactions with credit suppliers are recorded in both the purchases ledger control account in the general ledger and the suppliers' individual account in the subsidiary purchases ledger.

The purchases ledger contains a separate ledger account for each individual supplier. Every individual purchase invoice and cash payment is posted to an individual's account in the purchases ledger.

At the end of each period, the subsidiary ledgers are reconciled to check that the totals of the individual accounts are the same amounts showing in the sales ledger and purchases ledger control accounts.

2 Credit sales

2.1 Credit sales and the sales ledger

We have now looked at the three elements of a typical accounting system. We must now see how it all fits together.

We will first consider three credit sales invoices

Customer	Amount
A	£1,500
B	£2,000
C	£2,500

Step 1

Each invoice is recorded in the sales day book (SDB) and in the personal account of each customer in the sales ledger. The entry required for each invoice is a debit in each customer account to indicate that this is the amount that each one owes us.

Step 2

At the end of the period the sales day book is totalled and the total is entered into the sales ledger control account (SLCA) (total customers account) in the general ledger.

The full double entry is as we saw in the previous chapter (ignoring VAT):

Debit   Sales ledger control account

Credit   Sales

Step 3

Now consider the following cheques being received against these debts.

Customer	Amount
A	£1,000
B	£2,000

Each receipt is recorded in the cash book (see later chapter) and in the personal account of each customer in the sales ledger. The entry for cash received in the individual accounts is a credit entry to indicate that they no longer owe us these amounts.

Step 4

At the end of the period the cash book is totalled and the total is entered into the sales ledger control account (total customers account) in the general ledger.

The full double entry is:

Debit   Cash account (money in)

Credit   Sales ledger control account

This is illustrated on the next page.

Summary

1   The invoices are entered into the SDB and the cheques are entered into the cash book.

2   The totals from the cash book and SDB are posted to the SLCA.

3   The individual invoices and cash received are posted to the sales ledger.

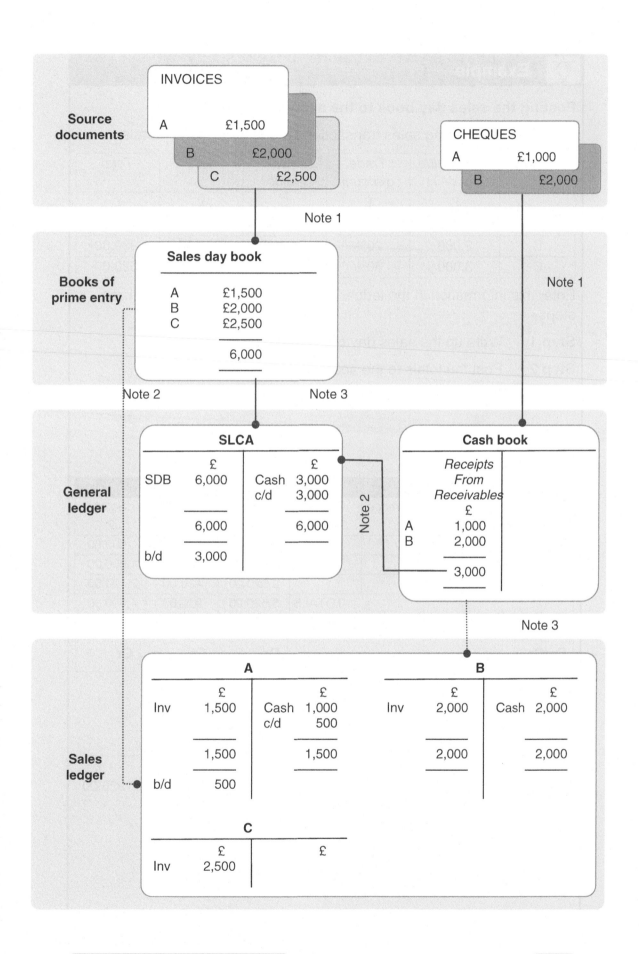

Example

Posting the sales day book to the accounts in the ledgers

Consider the following sales transactions made by Roberts Metals.

Customer	Sales value (ex VAT)	Trade discount	Net sales value	VAT	Total
	£	£	£	£	£
A	1,000	10%	900	180.00	1,080.00
B	2,000	20%	1,600	320.00	1,920.00
C	3,000	30%	2,100	420.00	2,520.00

Enter this information in the ledger accounts using the following three steps.

Step 1   Write up the sales day book, and total the columns.

Step 2   Post the totals to the accounts in the general ledger.

Step 3   Post the individual invoices to the sales ledger.

Solution

Step 1

SALES DAY BOOK

Date	Customer	Reference	Invoice number	Total £	VAT £	Sales £
	A			1,080.00	180.00	900.00
	B			1,920.00	320.00	1,600.00
	C			2,520.00	420.00	2,100.00
			TOTALS	5,520.00	920.00	4,600.00

Dr/Cr		Dr	Cr	Cr

Step 2

General ledger

Sales				VAT		
£		£			£	£
	SDB	4,600.00			SDB	920.00

SLCA			
	£		£
SDB	5,520.00		

Step 3

Sales ledger

A		B	
£	£	£	£
SDB 1,080.00		SDB 1,920.00	

C	
£	£
SDB 2,520.00	

Note to solution

(a) The totals of the SDB are entered in the general ledger.

(b) The individual invoices (total value including VAT) are entered in the individual customers accounts in the sales ledger. This is the amount that the customer will pay.

(c) Note that there are no entries for trade discounts either in the SDB or in the ledger accounts.

Activity 1

A sales day book has the following totals for a week.

Date	Invoice no	Customer name	Code	Total	VAT	Sales
				£	£	£
23/04/X0		Total		65,340	10,890	54,450
Dr/Cr						

Write the double entry for each column in the boxes above.

---

3 Sales returns

3.1 Recording transactions for returned goods

When customers return goods, the accounting system has to record the fact that goods have been returned. If the goods were returned following a cash sale then cash would be repaid to the customer.

If goods were returned following a credit sale then the SLCA in the general ledger and the customer's individual account in the sales ledger will need to be credited with the value of the goods returned.

 Example

Returns following a cash sale

X sells £500 of goods to A for cash plus £100 VAT

X subsequently agrees that A can return £200 worth of goods (excluding the VAT)

Record these transactions in the ledger accounts.

Solution

Step 1

First of all we need to set up a new account called the 'sales returns account' in the general ledger. This will be used in addition to the sales account and cash book with which you are familiar.

Step 2

Enter the cash sale in the accounts.

Debit bank account for cash received   £600.00
Credit sales with net amount   £500.00
Credit VAT account with VAT   £100.00

Bank account

	£		£
Sales	600.00		

Sales

	£		£
		Cash book	500.00

KAPLAN PUBLISHING

Sales returns

	£		£

VAT

	£		£
		Cash book	100.00

Step 3

X will repay A £200 plus VAT of (£200 × 20%) = £40. We therefore need to enter the sales return, the cash and the VAT in the accounts.

Debit sales returns account	£200.00
Debit VAT account £200 × 20%	£40.00
Credit bank account with cash paid out	£240.00

Bank account

	£		£
Sales	600.00	Sales returns	240.00

Sales

	£		£
		Cash book	500.00

Sales returns

	£		£
Cash book	200.00		

VAT

	£		£
Cash book	40.00	Cash book	100.00

3.2 Sales returns for credit sales – no VAT

When a credit customer returns goods, he does not receive cash for the return. Instead the seller will issue a credit note to record the fact that goods have been returned. The amount of the credit note will reduce the amount owed by the customer. This credit note is sent to the customer and is entered in the seller's books.

Example

X sells goods on credit to A for £500. A returns goods worth £200. X sends a credit note for £200 to A. Enter these transactions in the general ledger of X's books. There is no VAT.

Solution

Step 1

Record the invoice issued for the credit sale for £500:

Debit the SLCA in the general ledger with £500.

Credit the sales account in the general ledger with £500.

SLCA

	£		£
Sales	500.00		

Sales

	£		£
		SLCA	500.00

Step 2

Record the credit note for £200. The return is debited to a 'sales returns account' to reflect the reduction in sales. The SLCA is credited to show that the amount owed by the customer has been reduced.

SLCA

	£		£
Sales	500.00	Sales returns	200.00

Sales

	£		£
		SLCA	500.00

Sales returns

	£		£
SLCA	200.00		

3.3 Sales returns with VAT

When a return is made and we include VAT, the VAT has to be accounted for both on the invoice when the sale is made, and on the credit note when the goods are returned. This VAT has to be entered in the books.

> **Example**
>
> X sells goods on credit to B for £1,000 + VAT at 20%.
>
> B returns goods worth £400 + VAT at 20%.
>
> Enter these transactions in the general ledger of X's books.
>
> **Solution**
>
> **Step 1**
>
> Enter the invoice in the usual way, including the VAT.

SLCA

	£		£
Sales	1,200.00		

Sales

	£		£
		SLCA	1,000.00

VAT

	£		£
		SLCA	200.00

Step 2

Enter the credit note. The VAT on the return will be £400 × 20% = £80.

SLCA

	£		£
Sales	1,200.00	Sales returns	480.00

Sales

	£		£
		SLCA	1,000.00

VAT

	£		£
SLCA	80.00	SLCA	200.00

Sales returns

	£		£
SLCA	400.00		

The books will reflect the position after the return. The balance on the SLCA is £720. This is made up as:

	£
Sales	1,000
Sales return	400
	600
VAT 600 × 20%	120
	720

 Example

A and B are credit customers of Ellis Electricals. The balances on their accounts in the sales ledger are £1,200 and £2,400 (VAT inclusive amounts) because both A and B have made earlier purchases which have not yet been paid.

A returns goods which cost £600 excluding VAT. B returns goods which cost £400 excluding VAT.

Enter the above transactions in the sales returns day book and in the general and sales ledgers of Ellis Electricals.

Solution

Step 1

Enter the original sales invoices in the general ledger.

SLCA

	£			£
SDB	3,600.00			

Sales

	£			£
		SDB		3,000.00

VAT

	£			£
		SDB		600.00

A

	£		£
SDB	1,200.00		

B

	£		£
SDB	2,400.00		

Step 2

Write up the sales returns day book.

SALES RETURNS DAY BOOK						
Date	Customer	Reference	Credit note number	Total £	VAT £	Sales returns £
	A			720.00	120.00	600.00
	B			480.00	80.00	400.00
				1,200.00	200.00	1,000.00

Dr/Cr		Cr	Dr	Dr

Step 3

Enter the SRDB totals in the general ledger accounts.

SLCA

	£		£
SDB	3,600.00	SRDB	1,200.00

Sales

	£		£
		SDB	3,000.00

VAT

	£		£
SRDB	200.00	SDB	600.00

Sales returns

	£		£
SRDB	1,000.00		

Step 4

Enter the individual amounts in the sales ledger.

A

	£			£
SDB	1,200.00	SRDB		720.00

B

	£			£
SDB	2,400.00	SRDB		480.00

Activity 2

Given below are the totals of a sales returns day book for a week.

Date	Customer name	Credit note no	Code	Total	VAT	Sales returns
				£	£	£
23/04/X0				3,360	560	2,800

Dr/Cr						

Post these totals to the general ledger accounts.

4   Credit purchases

4.1   Introduction

When we studied accounting for sales earlier, we dealt with the three parts of the accounting records as they affected sales.

In the case of purchases, the parts are exactly the same except that instead of a 'sales day book' we have the 'purchases day book', and instead of the sales ledger we have the purchases ledger. The third part, namely the general ledger, is exactly the same and contains all the general ledger accounts with which you are familiar.

Remember that, as for sales, the double entry goes through the general ledger, and the purchases ledger is just a memorandum ledger that holds the details of the individual supplier's accounts (it is sometimes called the subsidiary (purchases) ledger).

On the next page we will illustrate how these parts fit together with a diagram.

4.2 Fitting it all together

Consider these three credit purchases invoices

Supplier	Amount
X	£4,000
Y	£5,000
Z	£6,000

Step 1

Each invoice is recorded in the purchases day book.

Step 2

At the end of the period the purchases day book is totalled and the total is entered into the purchases ledger control account in the general ledger. The individual entries are recorded in the individual supplier accounts in the purchases ledger.

Now consider these cheques being paid to the suppliers.

Customer	Amount
X	£2,000
Y	£3,000

Step 1

Each payment is recorded in the cash book.

Step 2

At the end of the period the cash book is totalled and the total is entered into the purchases ledger control account in the general ledger. The individual entries are recorded in the individual supplier accounts in the purchases ledger.

This is illustrated on the next page.

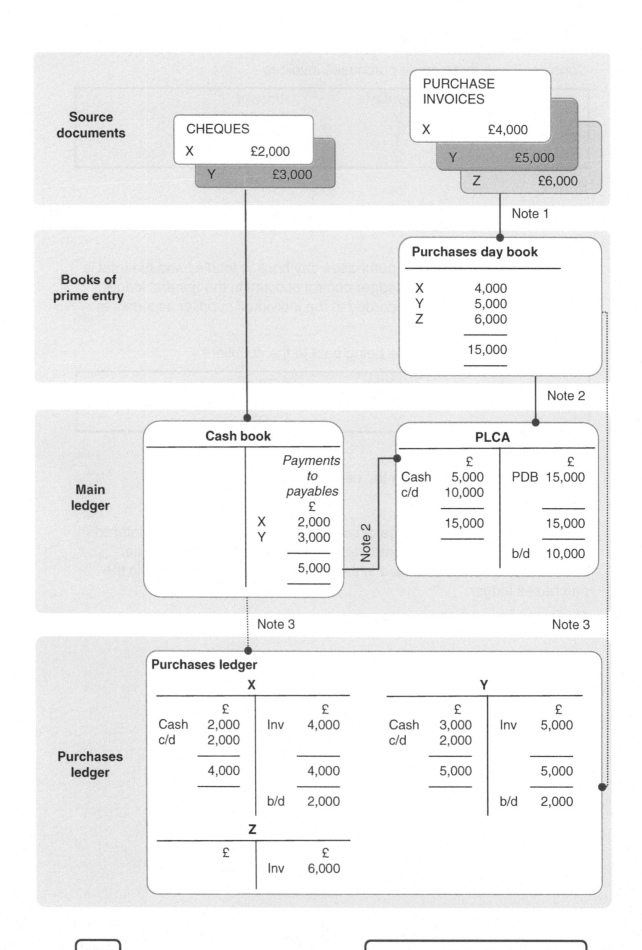

Summary

1   The invoices are entered into the PDB and the cheques are entered into the cash book.

2   The totals from the cash book and PDB are posted to the PLCA.

3   The individual invoices and cash received are posted to the purchases ledger.

 Example

Posting the purchases day book to the accounts in the ledgers

Consider the following purchase invoices received from suppliers by Roberts Metals.

Customer	Purchases value (ex VAT)	Trade discount	Net purchases value	VAT	Total
	£	£	£	£	£
X	500	10%	450.00	90.00	540.00
Y	1,750	20%	1,400.00	280.00	1,680.00
Z	5,000	30%	3,500.00	700.00	4,200.00

The following three steps are needed to enter this information in the ledger accounts.

Step 1   Write up the purchases day book, and total the columns.

Step 2   Post the totals to the accounts in the general ledger.

Step 3   Post the individual invoices to the purchases ledger.

Solution

Step 1

PURCHASES DAY BOOK

Date	Supplier	Reference	Invoice number	Total £	VAT £	Purchases £
	X			540.00	90.00	450.00
	Y			1,680.00	280.00	1,400.00
	Z			4,200.00	700.00	3,500.00
			TOTALS	6,420.00	1,070.00	5,350.00
Dr/Cr				Cr	Dr	Dr

Step 2

General ledger

Purchases				VAT			
	£		£		£		£
PDB	5,350.00			PDB	1,070.00		

PLCA			
	£		£
		PDB	6,420.00

Step 3

Purchases ledger

X				Y			
	£		£		£		£
		PDB	540.00			PDB	1,680.00

Z			
	£		£
		PDB	4,200.00

Note to solution

(a)   The totals of the PDB are entered in the general ledger.

(b)   The individual invoices (total value including VAT) are entered in the individual supplier accounts in the purchases ledger. This is the amount that will be paid to the supplier.

(c)   Note that there are no entries for trade discounts either in the PDB or in the ledger accounts.

Activity 3

Given below are the totals of a purchase day book for a week.

Date	Invoice no	Supplier	Code	Total	VAT	Purchases
				£	£	£
		Total		90,000	15,000	75,000

Dr/Cr			

How would the totals be posted to the general ledger accounts?

5 Purchases returns

5.1 Introduction

When a business buys and then returns goods to a supplier, the accounting system has to record the fact that goods have been returned. If the goods were returned following a cash purchase then cash would be repaid by the supplier to the customer who had bought the goods.

If goods were returned following a credit purchase then the PLCA in the general ledger will need to be debited and the individual supplier's account in the purchases ledger will need to be debited with the value of the goods returned to reduce the amount owed to the supplier. (We shall see the other entries required below).

 Example

Returns following a cash purchase

Y buys £1,000 of goods from B for cash plus £200 VAT (at 20% standard rated)

B subsequently agrees that Y can return £500 worth of goods (excluding VAT).

Record these transactions in the ledger accounts of Y.

Solution

Step 1

First of all we need to set up a new account called the 'purchases returns account' in the general ledger.

Step 2

Enter the cash purchases in the accounts of Y.

Credit cash book for cash paid	£1,200.00
Debit purchases with expense	£1,000.00
Debit VAT account with VAT	£200.00

Purchases

	£		£
Cash book	1,000.00		

Purchases returns

£		£

VAT

	£		£
Cash book	200		

Cash book

	£		£
		Purchases and VAT	1,200.00

Step 3

B will repay Y £500 plus VAT of £100. We therefore need to enter the purchases returns, the cash and the VAT in the accounts.

Cash book

	£		£
Purchases return + VAT	600.00	Purchases and VAT	1,200.00

Purchases

	£		£
Cash book	1,000.00		

Purchases returns

	£		£
		Cash book	500.00

VAT

	£		£
Cash book	200.00	Cash book	100.00

5.2 Purchases returns for credit purchases with VAT

When a credit customer returns goods, he does not receive cash for the return; the seller will issue a credit note to record the fact that goods have been returned. This credit note is sent to the customer and is entered in the customer's books.

When a return is made for goods that incur VAT, we include VAT; the VAT was accounted for on the invoice when the purchase was made, and now has to be accounted for on the credit note when the goods are returned. This VAT has to be entered in the books.

Example

D buys goods from Z for £800 + VAT at 20% (= £960).

D returns goods worth £200 + VAT at 20%.

Enter these transactions in the general ledger of D's books.

Solution

Step 1

Enter the invoice in the usual way, including the VAT.

PLCA

	£			£
		Purchases		960.00

Purchases

	£		£
PLCA	800.00		

VAT

	£		£
PLCA	160.00		

Step 2

Enter the credit note. The VAT on the return will be £200 × 20% = £40. This gives a total credit note of £240.

PLCA

	£		£
Purchases returns + VAT	240.00	Purchases	960.00

Purchases

	£		£
PLCA	800.00		

VAT

	£		£
PLCA	160.00	PLCA	40.00

Purchases returns

	£			£
			PLCA	200.00

The books will reflect the position after the return. The balance on the PLCA is £720. This is made up as:

	£
Purchase	800
Purchase return	(200)
	600
VAT 600 × 20%	120
	720

🔆 Example

John bought goods for £750 + VAT from X and £1,000 + VAT from Y.

John returns goods which cost £200 excluding VAT to X, and goods which cost £400 excluding VAT to Y.

Enter the above purchases and returns in the general and purchases ledger of John, using a purchases returns day book.

Solution

Step 1

Enter the original purchases invoices in the general ledger.

PLCA

	£			£
			PDB	2,100.00

Purchases

	£		£
PDB	1,750.00		

VAT

	£		£
PDB	350.00		

X

	£		£
		PDB (£750 + VAT)	900.00

Y

	£		£
		PDB (£1,000 + VAT)	1,200.00

Step 2

Write up the purchases returns day book.

PURCHASES RETURNS DAY BOOK						
Date	Supplier	Reference	Credit note number	Total £	VAT £	Purchases returns £
	X			240.00	40.00	200.00
	Y			480.00	80.00	400.00
				720.00	120.00	600.00

Dr/Cr		Dr	Cr	Cr

Step 3

Enter the PRDB totals in the general ledger accounts.

PLCA

	£		£
PRDB	720.00	PDB	2,100.00

Purchases

	£		£
PDB	1,750.00		

VAT

	£		£
PDB	350.00	PRDB	120.00

Purchases returns

	£		£
		PRDB	600.00

Step 4

Enter the individual amounts in the purchases ledger. The amounts will be debited to the individual supplier accounts as the return is reducing the amount that is owed to the supplier.

X			
	£		£
PRDB	240.00	PDB (£750 + VAT)	900.00

Y			
	£		£
PRDB	480.00	PDB (£1,000 + VAT)	1,200.00

Activity 4

Given below are the totals of a purchases returns day book for a week.

Date	Supplier	Credit note no	Code	Total	VAT	Purchase returns
				£	£	£
23/04/X0				9,600	1,600	8,000

Dr/Cr				

Post these totals to the general ledger accounts.

6 Summary and further questions

In this chapter we have reviewed how transactions are recorded.

Initially a transaction is recorded in the relevant book of prime entry (day book).

The double entry takes place in the general ledger, with the total of the gross sales being recorded in a sales ledger control account (SLCA) which we have previously called customers. The total of the gross purchases is recorded in a purchases ledger control account (PLCA) which we have previously called suppliers.

Subsidiary sales ledgers contain individual entries for individual customers whereas the subsidiary purchases ledgers contain individual entries for individual suppliers.

Below are further practice questions to test your knowledge of the above.

Activity 5

Below is a list of documents. Tick the box to which you think each belongs.

	Sales day book	Sales return day book	Purchase day book	Purchase returns day book	None of them
Sales invoice					
Purchase invoice					
Purchase credit note					
Remittance advice					
Sales credit note					

Activity 6

Your supervisor has gone on holiday and left you to transfer the purchase daybooks to the general ledger. You have been provided with the following information:

Date 20X5	Details	Invoice	Total	VAT	Net
	Total		910.44	151.74	758.70

a) Complete the appropriate boxes provided to ensure the correct double entry using the correct wording from the Pick list provided and debit and credit values

Statement	Debit	Credit

Pick list

Purchases	Sales return	Purchases return
VAT	Sales ledger control account	Purchase ledger control account

b) Is the following statement true or false?

Statement	True	False
The total will be a **credit** in the Purchase ledger		

Answers to chapter activities

 Activity 1

The required double entry is as follows:

Debit	Sales ledger control account	£65,340
Credit	VAT	£10,890
	Sales	£54,450

Note that it is the net amount that is credited to each sales account and the gross amount (including VAT) that is debited to the sales ledger control account. The VAT total is credited to the VAT account.

The ledger entries would appear as follows:

Sales ledger control account

	£		£
SDB	65,340		

VAT

	£			£
		SDB		10,890

Sales

	£			£
		SDB		54,450

Activity 2

Sales returns

	£		£
SRDB	2,800		

VAT account

	£		£
SRDB	560		

Sales ledger control account

	£		£
		SRDB	3,360

Note that it is the net amount that is debited to each returns account and the gross amount to the sales ledger control account. The difference, the VAT, is debited to the VAT account.

Activity 3

The required double entry is as follows:

Debit	VAT	£15,000
	Purchases	£75,000
Credit	Purchases ledger control account	£90,000

Note carefully that it is the net amount that is debited to each purchases account and the gross amount (including VAT) that is credited to the purchases ledger control account. The VAT total is debited to the VAT account.

The ledger entries would appear as follows:

Purchases ledger control account

	£		£
		PDB	90,000

VAT

	£		£
PDB	15,000		

Purchases

	£		£
PDB	75,000		

 Activity 4

Purchases returns – Department 1 account

	£		£
		PRDB	8,000

VAT account

	£		£
		PRDB	1,600

Purchases ledger control account

	£		£
PRDB	9,600		

Note that it is the net amount that is credited to each returns account and the gross amount to the purchases ledger control account. The difference, the VAT, is credited to the VAT account.

Activity 5

	Sales day book	Sales return day book	Purchase day book	Purchase returns day book	None of them
Sales invoice	✔				
Purchase invoice			✔		
Purchase credit note				✔	
Remittance advice					✔
Sales credit note		✔			

Activity 6

a)

Statement	Debit	Credit
Purchases	758.70	
VAT	151.74	
Purchase ledger control account		910.44

b)

Statement	True	False
The total will be a **credit** in the Purchase ledger	✔	

The cash book

Introduction

The Cash book is the organisation's record of all the money flowing into, and leaving the business. This chapter covers the transactions within the cash book.

KNOWLEDGE	CONTENTS
Bookkeeping and accounts	1 Recording cash receipts and cash payments
2 Be able to record cash and credit transactions in books of original entry	2 The cash book as part of the general ledger

1 Recording cash receipts and cash payments

1.1 Recording cash receipts

Definition

A cash book is a record of all monies received and paid by the business. The cash book can be used as a book of prime entry and also part of the double entry system acting as a ledger with monies received recorded on the debit side of the book and monies paid out recorded on the credit side of the book. If the cash book is used as a book of prime entry only, the transactions are transferred to a separate Cash Book or Bank account in the general ledger.

Example

The following is an example of the general and sales ledgers, including entries from the sales and sales returns day books.

General ledger

Sales

	£		£
		SDB	4,600.00

VAT

	£		£
SRDB	140.00	SDB	805.00

SLCA

	£		£
SDB	5,405.00	SRDB	940.00

Sales returns

	£		£
SRDB	800.00		

Sales ledger

A

	£		£
SDB	1,057.50		

B

	£		£
SDB	1,880.00		

C

	£		£
SDB	2,467.50	SRDB	940.00

The following transactions took place:

Customers A pays **£1,057.50**

Customers B pays **£1,000.00**

Enter this information in the cash receipts book and in the ledger accounts given above.

Solution

The following steps are needed.

Step 1 Enter these transactions in the cash book.

Step 2 Total the cash book and post the totals to the general ledger.

Step 3 Post the individual amounts of cash paid by customers to the individual accounts in the sales ledger.

Step 1

Date	Narrative	Reference	Total	VAT	SLCA	Cash sales
			£	£	£	£
	A		1,057.50	See Note 2	1,057.50	
	B		1,000.00	of Step 2	1,000.00	
		TOTALS	2,057.50		2,057.50	

Step 2

We have brought forward the balances from the general ledger in the earlier example and now post the cash received book (CRB) totals to the general ledger.

General ledger

Sales				VAT			
£		£		£		£	
		SDB	4,600.00	SRDB	140.00	SDB	805.00

SLCA				Sales returns			
£		£		£		£	
SDB	5,405.00	SRDB	940.00	SRDB	800.00		
		CRB	2,057.50				

Note 1: We have posted the total of the SLCA column of the CRB to the sales ledger control account. The entry to the sales ledger control account is a credit entry as this is reducing the amount owed by our customers.

Note 2: A common confusion is for people to wonder about the VAT – surely some of the money paid by A and B is actually paying the VAT part of the invoice. Yes it is, but we have already accounted for this VAT element when we entered the invoices themselves into the ledger accounts via the sales day book.

The total of the invoices in the SDB were debited to the SLCA and the VAT and sales were the corresponding credits. We therefore now post the total cash including VAT to the sales ledger control account but nothing is posted to the VAT account as this has already been done when dealing with the invoices.

Note 3: This is now the full double entry for the cash received completed.

Debit   Bank account (cash receipts book)

Credit   Sales ledger control account

We have credited the sales ledger control account and the entry in the cash receipts book itself is the related debit entry. So there is no need for any further debit entry.

Step 3

We have brought forward the balance from the sales ledger in the earlier example and now post the cash received to the individual sales ledger accounts. Again, as with the sales ledger control account, the amounts paid are credited to each customer as they reduce the amount owed by each customer.

A				B			
	£		£		£		£
b/f	1,057.50	CRB	**1,057.50**	b/f	1,880.00	CRB	**1,000.00**

C			
	£		£
b/f	2,467.50	SRDB	940.00

Activity 1

Below is the debit side of the cash book. The cash book is a book of prime entry **only**. There was no opening bank balance at the start of the month.

Cash book debit side

Details	Total	VAT	Sales ledger	Cash Sales
Totals	17,856	430	15,276	2,150

What would be the FOUR entries in the general ledger? Choose the account names from the Pick list provided.

Account name	Amount	Debit	Credit

Pick list

Bank

Purchase ledger

Purchase ledger control

Cash purchases

VAT

Sales ledger

Sales ledger control

Cash sales

Cash book

 Activity 2

Your organisation receives a number of cheques from customers through the post each day and these are listed on the cheque listing. It also makes some sales to non-credit customers each day which include VAT at the standard rate of 20% and are paid for by cheque.

Today's date is 28 April 20X1 and the cash receipts book is given below:

Date	Narrative	SL Code	Bank	SLCA	Sales	VAT 20%
20X1			£	£	£	£
28/4	G Heilbron	SL04	108.45	108.45		
	L Tessa	SL15	110.57	110.57		
	J Dent	SL17	210.98	210.98		
	F Trainer	SL21	97.60	97.60		
	A Winter	SL09	105.60	105.60		
	Cash Sales		270.72		225.60	45.12
	Total		**903.92**	**633.20**	**225.60**	**45.12**

Required:

Show what the entries in the sales ledger will be:

Account name	Amount £	Dr ✓	Cr ✓

Show what the entries in the general ledger will be:

Account name	Amount £	Dr ✓	Cr ✓

1.2 Recording cash payments

The Purchases Day Book (PDB) is often used only for invoices from suppliers of purchases, i.e. goods for resale. Invoices for rent, electricity, telephone and similar items will typically not be entered in the PDB. They will be paid by cheque, and the double entry will be made directly between the cash payments book and the relevant expense account in the general ledger.

The reason for this is that the purchases day book (like the sales day book) is used to record purchases made on credit. Purchases of goods made on cash terms will be recorded in the cash book. Payment of expenses also tend to be on a cash basis and therefore will be recorded in the cash book.

 Example

Parma Products buys goods for resale from two suppliers on credit. The business buys £1,000 + VAT at 20% of goods from X and £3,000 + VAT at 20% of goods from Y.

Parma also buys goods for resale from a retail supplier with whom he does not have credit terms, and pays for the goods, £500 + VAT at 20%, at the till. Parma also pays X's invoice in full.

Enter these transactions in the accounts of Parma Products. The cash purchase is not entered in the PDB.

Solution

Step 1   Enter the invoices for goods in the PDB.

PURCHASES DAY BOOK

Date	Supplier	Reference	Invoice number	Total £	VAT £	Purchases £
	X			1,200	200	1,000
	Y			3,600	600	3,000
			TOTALS	4,800	800	4,000

Step 2 Enter the totals of the PDB in the general ledger.

Purchases

	£		£
PDB	4,000.00		

VAT

	£		£
PDB	800.00		

PLCA

	£		£
		PDB	4,800.00

Step 3 Enter the cash paid in the analysed cash payments book.

Date	Narrative	Reference	Total	VAT	PLCA	Cash purchase
			£	£	£	£
	X		1,200.00		1,200.00	
	Cash purchase		600.00	100.00		500.00
		TOTALS	1,800.00	**100.00**	1,200.00	**500.00**

Note that the VAT on the payment to the supplier has already been accounted for in the general ledger via the entries in the PDB. However, the cash purchase was not entered in the PDB and so the VAT has to be entered in the VAT column of the cash book from where it will be posted to the VAT account (see Step 4).

Step 4 Post the cash paid totals from the cash book to the general ledger.

Purchases

	£		£
PDB	4,000.00		
CPB	**500.00**		

VAT

	£		£
PDB	800.00		
CPB	**100.00**		

PLCA

	£		£
CPB	1,200.00	PDB	4,800.00

Note 1: All the VAT paid is now debited to the VAT account. You must make sure that you understand how some is posted via the PDB and some via the cash book.

Note 2: All of the entries made from the cash payments book are debit entries. The credit entry is the total of the cash payments (£1,800) since the cash payments book is part of the double entry.

Step 5: Enter the amounts in the purchases ledger.

X

	£		£
CPB	1,200.00	PDB	1,200.00

Y

	£		£
		PDB	3,600.00

The entries to the purchases ledger from the cash payments book are debit entries in the individual Supplier accounts as the payment means that less is owed to the Supplier.

2 The cash book as part of the general ledger

2.1 The cash book in the assessment

The assessment may show the cashbook as a ledger account format. This means that the cashbook actually forms a part of the general ledger, with the entries being one side of the double entry required within the general ledger.

Therefore a typical assessment requirement will be to complete the other side of the entry within the general ledger, and to update the individual accounts in the subsidiary ledger.

Example

Date	Detail	Bank £	Date	Detail	Bank £
30/6/X9	Bal b/d	16,173	30/6/X9	Supplier P	5,500
30/6/X9	Customer A	13,200	30/6/X9	Cash purchase	1,500
			30/6/X9	Bal c/d	22,373
		29,373			**29,373**

We need to appreciate that the bank account has already been completed with one side of the entries, and the other side of the entry is all that is required to complete the double entry postings.

It is also important to note that the discount column is still to be treated as a memorandum column, requiring both the debit and the credit entries.

Postings to general ledger (ignoring VAT)

Account	Amount	Dr or Cr
SLCA	13,200	Cr
PLCA	5,500	Dr
Purchases	1,500	Dr

Postings to the sales ledger

Account	Amount	Dr or Cr
Customer A account	13,200	Cr

Postings to the purchase ledger

Account	Amount	Dr or Cr
Supplier P	5,500	Dr

 Activity 3

Below is the debit side of the cash book. The cash book is a book of prime entry **and** part of the double entry bookkeeping system. There was no opening bank balance at the start of the month

Cash book debit side

Details	Total	VAT	Sales ledger	Cash Sales
Totals	17,856	430	15,276	2,150

What would be the THREE entries in the general ledger? Choose the account names from the Pick list provided.

Account name	Amount	Debit	Credit

Pick list

Bank	Cash book	Cash purchases
Purchase ledger	Purchase ledger control	Cash sales
Sales ledger	Sales ledger control	VAT

Activity 4

Date	Detail	Bank £	Date	Detail	Bank £
30/6/X9	Bal b/d	24,067	30/6/X9	Cash purchase	20,000
			30/6/X9	Supplier B	2,500
			30/6/X9	Bal c/d	1,567
		24,067			**24,067**
1/7/X9	Bal b/d	1,567			

What are the postings to the general and purchases ledgers based on the accounts above?

Postings to general ledger (ignoring VAT)

Account	Amount	Dr or Cr

Postings to the purchase ledger

Account	Amount	Dr or Cr

📝 Activity 5

You may be asked to only record transactions for one side of the cash book.

Cashbook – debit side

Details	Bank £
Balance b/f	2,568
Edwards Ltd	3,864
Andrews Associates	4,223

(a)   Record the TWO transactions within the sales ledger.

(b)   Record the ONE transaction within the general ledger.

It is important to appreciate that the above is still the cashbook as a ledger account, but only one half is required. Therefore, the entries will be the same as previously shown.

a)   **Sales ledger**

Details	Amount £	Debit/Credit

b)   **General ledger**

Details	Amount £	Debit/Credit

Activity 6

Cashbook – credit side

Details	VAT £	Bank £
Cash purchases	60	360
PLCA		4,785

Record the THREE transactions provided within the general ledger.

Details	Amount £	Debit/Credit

 Activity 7

Tick the statements below which you think are correct.

Statement	True	False
The cash book is a book of prime entry ONLY		
The credit side of the cash book is for money paid INTO the business		
A customer receipt of £250.00 is credited to the Sales ledger control account and debited to the Purchase ledger		
A customer receipt is debited to the cash book and credited to the Sales ledger control account		
The VAT showing on the credit side of the cash book is the VAT calculated on cash purchases ONLY		
A supplier payment is debited to the Purchase ledger control account and also to the purchase ledger		

Answers to chapter activities

📝 Activity 1

Account name	Amount	Debit	Credit
Cash book	17,856	✔	
VAT	430		✔
Sales ledger control	15,276		✔
Cash sales	2,150		✔

📝 Activity 2

Account name	Amount £	Dr ✔	Cr ✔
G Heilbron	108.45		✔
L Tessa	110.57		✔
J Dent	210.98		✔
F Trainer	97.60		✔
A Winter	105.60		✔

Account name	Amount £	Dr ✔	Cr ✔
SLCA	633.20		✔
Sales	225.60		✔
VAT	45.12		✔

Activity 3

Account name	Amount	Debit	Credit
VAT	430		✔
Sales ledger control	15,276		✔
Cash sales	2,150		✔

Activity 4

Postings to general ledger (ignoring VAT)

Account	Amount	Dr or Cr
Purchases	20,000	Dr
PLCA	2,500	Dr

Postings to the purchase ledger

Account	Amount	Dr or Cr
Supplier B account	2,500	Dr

Activity 5

a) **Sales ledger**

Details	Amount £	Debit/Credit
Edwards Ltd	3,864	Cr
Andrews Associates	4,223	Cr

b) **General ledger**

Details	Amount £	Debit/Credit
SLCA	8,087	Cr

Activity 6

Details	Amount (£)	Debit/Credit
Cash purchases	300	DR
VAT	60	DR
PLCA	4,785	DR

Activity 7

Statement	True	False
The cash book is a book of prime entry ONLY		✔
The credit side of the cash book is for money paid INTO the business		✔
A customer receipt of £250.00 is credited to the Sales ledger control account and debited to the Purchase ledger		✔
A customer receipt is debited to the cash book and credited to the Sales ledger control account	✔	
The VAT showing on the credit side of the cash book is the VAT calculated on cash purchases ONLY	✔	
A supplier payment is debited to the Purchase ledger control account and also to the purchase ledger	✔	

Petty cash

9

Introduction

This chapter considers petty cash and explains why a business may need it and how to account for it.

KNOWLEDGE	CONTENTS
Bookkeeping and accounts	1 Petty cash payments and vouchers
4 Be able to understand the petty cash imprest system	2 The imprest system
	3 Posting petty cash
	4 Reconciling the petty cash
	5 End of chapter questions

1 Petty cash payments and vouchers

1.1 What is petty cash?

 Definition

Petty cash is the small amount of cash that most businesses hold in order to make small cash payments, such as payment for coffee and milk for the staff kitchen.

1.2 Petty cash box

Holding cash on business premises is a security risk and therefore it is important that the petty cash is secure. It should be kept in a locked petty cash box and usually this itself will be held in the safe.

Only the person responsible for the petty cash should have access to the petty cash box.

1.3 Payment of petty cash

Petty cash is usually reimbursed to employees who have already incurred a small cash expense on behalf of the business. These payments should be made for valid business expenses only.

For this reason, the petty cashier should pay out to the employee on receipt of an authorised petty cash voucher and, where appropriate, VAT receipt.

 Definition

A petty cash voucher is an internal document that details the business expenditure that an employee has incurred out of his own money.

This voucher must be authorised by an appropriate person before any amounts can be paid to that employee out of the petty cash box.

A typical petty cash voucher is shown below.

Signature of person authorising voucher

PETTY CASH VOUCHER				
Authorised by F R Clarke	Received by L Kent		No	4173
Date	Description		Amount	
4 April 20X1	Train Fare		12	50
Total			12	50

Signature of claimant

Sequential voucher number

Details of expenditure including the date and the nature of the expense

Total paid to employee

1.4 Maintaining petty cash records

The cashier, on receipt of the petty cash voucher should check that the receipt is genuine and that the voucher amounts add up to the total. Once the petty cash vouchers have been received, checked, authorised and the employee reimbursed, the details are recorded in the petty cash book. Earlier in this book we were briefly introduced to the petty cash book as a book of prime entry. In this chapter we will look how petty cash transactions are recorded in the petty cash book.

1.5 Writing up the petty cash book

When cash is paid into the petty cash book it will be recorded on the receipts side (debit side) of the petty cash book.

Each petty cash voucher will then in turn be written up in the petty cash book on the payments (credit) side.

To ensure that no vouchers have been mislaid, petty cash vouchers are pre-numbered sequentially.

Each voucher is then entered into the petty cash book in the correct order, with each item of expenditure being recorded in the correct expense analysis column.

💡 Example

A business has just started to run a petty cash system with an amount of £100. £100 is withdrawn from the bank account and paid into the petty cash box on *3* April 20X1.

During the first week the following authorised petty cash vouchers were paid. These transactions will now be recorded in the petty cash book.

PETTY CASH VOUCHER

Authorised by T Smedley	Received by P Lannall	No	0001	
Date	Description		Amount	
3 April 20X1	Tea/coffee/milk		4	73
	Total		4	73

PETTY CASH VOUCHER

Authorised by T Smedley	Received by R Sellers	No	0002	
Date	Description		Amount	
3 April 20X1	Train fare		14	90
	Total		14	90

PETTY CASH VOUCHER

Authorised by T Smedley	Received by F Dorne	No	0003	
Date	Description		Amount	
4 April 20X1	Stationery		4	00
	VAT		0	80
	Total		4	80

PETTY CASH VOUCHER

Authorised by T Smedley	Received by P Dent	No	0004	
Date	Description		Amount	
5 April 20X1	Postage costs		16	35
	Total		16	35

PETTY CASH VOUCHER

Authorised by	Received by	No	0005
T Smedley	H Polly		
Date	Description	Amount	
7 April 20X1	Train fare	15	30
	Total	15	30

PETTY CASH VOUCHER

Authorised by	Received by	No	0006
T Smedley	P Lannall		
Date	Description	Amount	
8 April 20X1	Milk/biscuits	3	85
	Total	3	85

Solution

Petty cash book											
Receipts			**Payments**								
Date	Narrative	Total	Date	Narrative	Voucher no	Total	Postage	Travel	Tea & coffee	Sundry	VAT
20X1		£	20X1			£	£	£	£	£	£
03/04	Cash	100.00	03/04	Tea/coffee	0001	4.73			4.73		
			03/04	Train fare	0002	14.90		14.90			
			04/04	Stationery	0003	4.80				4.00	0.80
			05/04	Postage	0004	16.35	16.35				
			07/04	Train fare	0005	15.30		15.30			
			08/04	Milk/biscuits	0006	3.85			3.85		

2 The imprest system

2.1 The use of an imprest system

Many businesses use the imprest system for petty cash. Using an imprest system makes petty cash easier to control and therefore reduces the possibility of error and fraud.

An imprest system is where a business decides on a fixed amount of petty cash (the imprest) which is just large enough to cover normal petty cash expenditure for a period of time decided by the management of the business (usually a week or a month). This amount of petty cash is withdrawn from the bank.

Claims are paid out of petty cash by a voucher being completed for each amount of petty cash paid out. The vouchers are kept in the petty cash box so that the amount of cash held decreases and is replaced by vouchers.

At any given time, the total contents of the box (i.e. petty cash plus amounts withdrawn represented by vouchers) should equal the amount of the imprest.

At the end of the period, a cheque is drawn for the total of the vouchers which restores the petty cash float to the amount of the imprest. The vouchers are removed from the petty cash box and filed.

 Example

The imprest amount for a petty cash system is £150, which is the amount paid into the petty cash box on 1 March. At the end of the week the total of the vouchers in the petty cash box is £125.05. How much cash is required to replenish the petty cash box to the imprest amount?

Solution

£125.05, the amount paid out on the basis of the petty cash vouchers.

2.2 Non-imprest petty cash system

An imprest petty cash system as in the previous example is the most common method of dealing with and controlling petty cash. However, some businesses may use a non-imprest system. This is where a set amount of cash is withdrawn every so often and paid into the petty cash box no matter what the level of expenditure in that week.

For example it may be an organisation's policy to cash a cheque for £50 each Monday morning for use as petty cash for the week. The danger here is either that petty cash requirements are more than £50 in the week in which case the petty cash box will run out of money. It could also be that week after week expenditure is a lot less than £50 each week, leading to a large amount of cash building up in the petty cash box.

3 Posting petty cash

3.1 Posting the petty cash book

Now that the petty cash book has been written up, we must now post the totals of the petty cash book to the general ledger accounts.

The petty cash book, like the cash book, can either be used either just as a prime entry with postings made to a petty cash account in the general ledger, or a book of prime entry and as a ledger account forming part of the double entry bookkeeping system.

3.2 Posting the petty cash receipt

The receipt into the petty cash box has come from cash being withdrawn from the bank account. This will have been done by writing out a cheque for cash and it from the bank. Therefore, the cheque should be recorded in the cash payments book as a payment (credit) when the cash payments book is written up and as a receipt (debit) when the petty cash book is written up.

3.3 Posting the petty cash payments

We will consider an example where the petty cash book is part of the double entry bookkeeping system as well as being a book of prime entry.

Example

A petty cash book to be posted to the general ledger accounts:

Petty cash book											
Receipts			Payments								
Date	Narrative	Total	Date	Narrative	Voucher no	Total	Postage	Travel	Tea & coffee	Sundry	VAT
20X1		£	20X1			£	£	£	£	£	£
20/08	Bal b/d	100.00	20/08	Tea/coffee	0001	13.68			13.68		
20/08	Bank	50.00	21/08	Train fare	0002	6.80		6.80			
			21/08	Stationery	0003	19.20				16.00	3.20
			22/08	Postage	0004	16.35	16.35				
			23/08	Train fare	0005	15.30		15.30			
			24/08	Milk/biscuits	0006	3.85			3.85		

Solution

Step 1 Each of the columns in the petty cash payments side must be totalled.

Petty cash book											
Receipts			Payments								
Date	Narrative	Total	Date	Narrative	Voucher no	Total	Postage	Travel	Tea & coffee	Sundry	VAT
20X1		£	20X1			£	£	£	£	£	£
20/08	Bal b/d	100.00	20/08	Tea/coffee	0001	13.68			13.68		
20/08	Bank	50.00	21/08	Train fare	0002	6.80		6.80			
			21/08	Stationery	0003	19.20				16.00	3.20
			22/08	Postage	0004	16.35	16.35				
			23/08	Train fare	0005	15.30		15.30			
			24/08	Milk/biscuits	0006	3.85			3.85		
25/08	Bal b/d	150.00		Totals		75.18	16.35	22.10	17.53	16.00	3.20

Check the totals:

	£
Postage	16.35
Travel	22.10
Tea and coffee	17.53
Sundry	16.00
VAT	3.20
	___
Total	75.18

Step 2 Each of the analysis column totals must now be entered into the general ledger accounts as debit entries.

VAT account

	£		£
Petty cash book (PCB)	3.20		

The entry has come from the petty cash book and this is the reference – this is now shortened to PCB.

Postage account

	£		£
PCB	16.35		

Travel account

	£		£
PCB	22.10		

Tea and coffee account

	£		£
PCB	17.53		

Sundry expenses account

	£		£
PCB	16.00		

Bank account

	£		£
		PCB	50.00

The balancing amount of £74.82 should represent the cash that is now in the petty cash tin (£150-75.18).

There is no need for an entry to the petty cash control account as the petty cash book acts as the general ledger account and the closing balance on the account is taken from it when the trial balance is prepared (£74.82 closing Petty cash balance).

3.4 Where the petty cash book is not part of the double entry bookkeeping system

When the petty cash book is not part of the double entry system, the accounting entries must show the impact on the expense accounts, the VAT account and the petty cash control account.

In the event of there being a top up to the petty cash, a separate entry will be required. We would need to show the money being withdrawn from the bank and deposited into petty cash.

We will now consider the earlier illustration to review the general ledger postings required when the petty cash book is not part of the double entry accounting system.

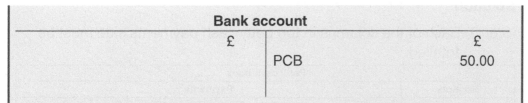

Example

A petty cash book is give below. This is to be posted to the general ledger accounts.

Petty cash book											
Receipts			**Payments**								
Date	Narrative	Total	Date	Narrative	Voucher no	Total	Postage	Travel	Tea & coffee	Sundry	VAT
20X1		£	20X1			£	£	£	£	£	£
20/08	Bal b/d	100.00	20/08	Tea/coffee	0001	13.68			13.68		
20/08	Bank	50.00	21/08	Train fare	0002	6.80		6.80			
			21/08	Stationery	0003	19.20				16.00	3.20
			22/08	Postage	0004	16.35	16.35				
			23/08	Train fare	0005	15.30		15.30			
			24/08	Milk/biscuits	0006	3.85			3.85		

Solution

Step 1 Each of the columns in the petty cash payments side must be totalled.

Petty cash book											
Receipts			**Payments**								
Date	Narrative	Total	Date	Narrative	Voucher no	Total	Postage	Travel	Tea & coffee	Sundry	VAT
20X1		£	20X1			£	£	£	£	£	£
20/08	Bal b/d	100.00	20/08	Tea/coffee	0001	13.68			13.68		
20/08	Bank	50.00	21/08	Train fare	0002	6.80		6.80			
			21/08	Stationery	0003	19.20				16.00	3.20
			22/08	Postage	0004	16.35	16.35				
			23/08	Train fare	0005	15.30		15.30			
			24/08	Milk/biscuits	0006	3.85			3.85		
				Bal c/d		74.82					
		150.00				150.00					
25/08	Bal b/d	74.82					16.35	22.10	17.53	16.00	3.20

Check the totals:

Dr/Cr	Cr	Dr	Dr	Dr	Dr	Dr

	£
Postage	16.35
Travel	22.10
Tea and coffee	17.53
Sundry	16.00
VAT	3.20
Total	75.18

We have been told that the petty cash book is not part of the double entry accounting system. The expense accounts of postage, travel, tea and coffee, sundry and the VAT account will be debited; the impact on the petty cash control account will be to credit it (to reduce the balance) by £75.18 in total that has been paid out.

Remember that the account name in the general ledger should always match the analysis column headings in the petty cash-book and not the description of the expense given in the 'Details' column.

We must also record the impact of the top-up to the petty cash from the bank account. This will be shown as a credit from the bank ledger account and a debit to the petty cash control account.

Step 2   We will now make the entries required into the general ledger accounts

VAT account

	£		£
Petty cash book (PCB)	3.20		

The entry has come from the petty cash book and this is the reference – this is now shortened to PCB.

Postage account

	£		£
PCB	16.35		

Travel account

	£		£
PCB	22.10		

Tea and coffee account

	£		£
PCB	17.53		

Sundry expenses account

	£		£
PCB	16.00		

Bank account

	£		£
		PCB	50.00

Petty cash control

	£		£
Balance b/d	100.00	PCB	75.18
Bank	50.00		

Activity 1

Summary of petty cash vouchers in hand at 31 October 20X7

Date	Description	Total £	VAT incl £
1/10	Envelopes (Administration)	19.72	3.28
4/10	Cleaner (Administration)	8.75	
6/10	Food for staff lunch (Marketing)	17.13	
6/10	Taxi fares (Marketing)	16.23	
6/10	Rail fares (Marketing)	43.75	
10/10	Postage (Administration)	4.60	
15/10	Tea and coffee (Production)	4.39	
17/10	Light bulbs and refuse sacks (Distribution)	8.47	1.41
20/10	Flowers for reception (Administration)	21.23	
26/10	Cleaner (Administration)	8.75	

(a) Write up the payments side of the petty cash book for October 20X7 from this information using the blank petty cash book below.

You should allocate a sequential voucher number to each entry in the petty cash book. The last voucher number to be allocated in September was 6578.

(b) Total each column in the petty cash book and cross-cast them.

PETTY CASH BOOK – PAYMENTS						
Date	Voucher no	Total	Production	Distribution	Marketing	Administration	VAT
		£	£	£	£	£	£

(c) Post the totals to the general ledger accounts given.

Production expenses account

£		£

Distribution expenses account

£		£

Marketing expenses account

£		£

Administration expenses account

£		£

VAT account

£		£

4 Reconciling the petty cash

4.1 Reconciling the petty cash

We saw earlier in the chapter that when an imprest system is being used for petty cash then at any point in time the amount of cash in the petty cash box plus the total of the vouchers in the petty cash box should equal the imprest amount.

At regular intervals, usually at the end of each week, this check will be carried out.

4.2 Procedure for reconciling the petty cash box

The total amount of cash in the petty cash box will be counted. The vouchers that have been paid during the week are also in the petty cash box and they must also be totalled.

When the amount of cash is added to the total of the vouchers in the box they should equal the imprest amount.

The petty cash vouchers for the week will then be removed from the box and filed.

 Example

The amount of cash remaining in a petty cash box at the end of a week is as follows:

Notes/coins	Quantity
£10	1
£5	2
£2	3
£1	7
50p	9
20p	11
10p	15
5p	7
2p	16
1p	23

The imprest amount is £100 and the vouchers in the petty cash box at the end of the week are as follows:

PETTY CASH VOUCHER				
Authorised by C Alexi	Received by P Trant	No	0467	
Date	Description		Amount	
4 May 20X3	Window cleaner		15	00
		Total	15	00

PETTY CASH VOUCHER				
Authorised by C Alexi	Received by F Saint	No	0468	
Date	Description		Amount	
5 May 20X3	Train fare		9	80
		Total	9	80

PETTY CASH VOUCHER

Authorised by C Alexi	Received by A Paul	No	0469	
Date	Description		Amount	
5 May 20X3	Stationery		8	00
	VAT		1	40
	Total		9	40

PETTY CASH VOUCHER

Authorised by C Alexi	Received by P Peters	No	0470	
Date	Description		Amount	
7 May 20X3	Postage		6	80
	Total		6	80

PETTY CASH VOUCHER

Authorised by C Alexi	Received by C Ralph	No	0471	
Date	Description		Amount	
5 May 20X3	Train fare		16	90
	Total		16	90

The cash and vouchers in the petty cash box at the end of the week are to be reconciled.

Solution

The petty cash must be totalled:

Notes/coins	Quantity	Amount (£)
£10	1	10.00
£5	2	10.00
£2	3	6.00
£1	7	7.00
50p	9	4.50
20p	11	2.20
10p	15	1.50
5p	7	0.35
2p	16	0.32
1p	23	0.23
		42.10

Now the vouchers must be totalled.

	£
0467	15.00
0468	9.80
0469	9.40
0470	6.80
0471	16.90
	57.90

Finally, total the cash and the vouchers to ensure that they add back to the imprest amount.

	£
Cash	42.10
Vouchers	57.90
	100.00

 Activity 2

Your business runs a petty cash box based upon an imprest amount of £60. This morning you have emptied the petty cash box and found the following notes, coins and vouchers.

Notes		Coins		Vouchers	
Value	Quantity	Value	Quantity	No	£
£5	2	£1	3	2143	10.56
		50p	5	2144	3.30
		20p	4	2145	9.80
		10p	6	2146	8.44
		5p	7	2147	2.62
		2p	10	2148	6.31
		1p	8	2149	1.44

Required:

Reconcile the cash and the vouchers in the petty cash box.

Activity 3

Given below is a business' petty cash book for the week.

Petty cash book											
Receipts			Payments								
Date	Narrative	Total	Date	Details	Voucher no	Amount	Postage	Staff welfare	Station-ery	Travel expenses	VAT
						£	£	£	£	£	£
5/1/X1	Bal b/d	150.00	12/1/X1	Postage	03526	13.68	13.68				
				Staff welfare	03527	25.00		25.00			
				Stationery	03528	15.12			12.60		2.52
				Taxi fare	03529	12.25				10.21	2.04
				Staff welfare	03530	6.40		6.40			
				Postage	03531	12.57	12.57				
				Rail fare	03532	6.80				6.80	
				Stationery	03533	8.16			6.80		1.36
				Taxi fare	03534	19.20				16.00	3.20
				Bal c/d		30.82					
		150.00				150.00					
25/08	Bal b/d	30.82					26.25	31.40	19.40	33.01	9.12

Required:

The Petty Cash Book is part of the double entry bookkeeping system.

Show what the entries in the general ledger will be:

Account name	Amount £	Dr ✓	Cr ✓

5   End of chapter questions

Activity 4

a)   Below is a statement about petty cash. Carefully read the statement and tick the box that you think is most appropriate.

Statement	Correct	Incorrect
Petty cash is used for buying very expensive purchases		

b)   Below is a list of different types of organisations. Which of the organisations do you think would deal mainly with cash? Tick the box you think is correct.

Organisation	Yes	No
A newsagent		
A business trading with many different countries and currencies		
A market stall		
A business that buys and sells on credit terms		

c)   Below are some statements. Carefully read the statements and tick the box that you think is correct.

Statement	Correct	Incorrect
An imprest system is one where the petty cash is topped up to a set amount at regular intervals		
The petty cash box can be left out in the office, as everyone is very honest and trustworthy		
If the balance on the petty cash imprest system should be £100.00, and there are vouchers totalling £53.60, then the amount needed to top up the petty cash is £46.40		
VAT cannot be claimed on purchases made via petty cash		
The petty cash book can be a book of prime entry AND part of the double entry bookkeeping system		
You are reconciling the petty cash. You find that though there should be £46.40 in cash in the box, there is only £45.20. Your supervisor says it doesn't matter		

KAPLAN PUBLISHING

Answers to chapter activities

 ## Activity 1

(a), (b)

Date	Voucher no	Total £		Production £		Distribution £		Marketing £		Administration £		VAT £	
PETTY CASH BOOK – PAYMENTS													
01/10/X7	6579	19	72							16	44	3	28
04/10/X7	6580	8	75							8	75		
06/10/X7	6581	17	13					17	13				
06/10/X7	6582	16	23					16	23				
06/10/X7	6583	43	75					43	75				
10/10/X7	6584	4	60							4	60		
15/10/X7	6585	4	39	4	39								
17/10/X7	6586	8	47			7	06					1	41
20/10/X7	6587	21	23							21	23		
26/10/X7	6588	8	75							8	75		
		153	02	4	39	7	06	77	11	59	77	4	69

(c)

Production expenses account

	£		£
PCB	4.39		

Distribution expenses account

	£		£
PCB	7.06		

Marketing expenses account

	£		£
PCB	77.11		

Administration expenses account

	£		£
PCB	59.77		

VAT account

	£		£
PCB	4.69		

Activity 2

Notes and coins

	£	£
£5 × 2	10.00	
£1 × 3	3.00	
50p × 5	2.50	
20p × 4	0.80	
10p × 6	0.60	
5p × 7	0.35	
2p × 10	0.20	
1p × 8	0.08	
		17.53

Vouchers

	£	£
2143	10.56	
2144	3.30	
2145	9.80	
2146	8.44	
2147	2.62	
2148	6.31	
2149	1.44	
		42.47
Imprest amount		60.00

Activity 3

The entries in the general ledger will be:

Account name	Amount £	Dr ✓	Cr ✓
Postage	26.25	✓	
Staff Welfare	31.40	✓	
Stationery	19.40	✓	
Travel Expenses	33.01	✓	
VAT	9.12	✓	

KAPLAN PUBLISHING

Activity 4

a)

Statement	Correct	Incorrect
Petty cash is used for buying very expensive purchases		✓

b)

Organisation	Yes	No
A newsagent	✓	
A business trading with many different countries and currencies		✓
A market stall	✓	
A business that buys and sells on credit terms		✓

c)

Statement	Correct	Incorrect
An imprest system is one where the petty cash is topped up to a set amount at regular intervals	✓	
The petty cash box can be left out in the office, as everyone is very honest and trustworthy		✓
If the balance on the petty cash imprest system should be £100.00, and there are vouchers totalling £53.60, then the amount needed to top up the petty cash is £46.40	✓	
VAT cannot be claimed on purchases made via petty cash		✓
The petty cash book can be a book of prime entry AND part of the double entry bookkeeping system	✓	
You are reconciling the petty cash. You find that though there should be £46.40 in cash in the box, there is only £45.20. Your supervisor says it doesn't matter		✓

Bank reconciliations

Introduction

Completion of this chapter will ensure we are able to correctly prepare the cash book, compare the entries in the cash book to details on the bank statement and then finally to prepare a bank reconciliation statement. We will explore the concept of the bank reconciliation, producing an updated cash book using this knowledge.

KNOWLEDGE
Bookkeeping and accounts
3.1 Update a cash book (bank balance) using details from a bank statement.
3.2 Recalculate the closing bank balance.
3.3 Be able to prepare bank reconciliations.

CONTENTS

1 Writing up the cash book

1.1 Introduction

Most businesses will have a separate cash receipts book and a cash payments book which form part of the double entry system. If this form of record is used, the cash balance must be calculated from the opening balance at the beginning of the period, plus the receipts shown in the cash receipts book for the period and minus the payments shown in the cash payments book for the period.

1.2 Balancing the cash book

The following brief calculation will enable us to find the balance on the cash book when separate receipts and payments book are maintained.

	£
Opening balance per the cash book	X
Add: Receipts in the period	X
Less: Payments in the period	(X)
Closing balance per the cash book	X

 Example

Suppose that the opening balance on the cash book is £358.72 on 1 June. During June the cash payments book shows that there were total payments made of £7,326.04 during the month of June and the cash receipts book shows receipts for the month of £8,132.76.

What is the closing balance on the cash book at the end of June?

Solution

		£
Opening balance at 1 June		358.72
Add:	Receipts for June	8,132.76
Less:	Payments for June	(7,326.04)
Balance at 30 June		1,165.44

Activity 1

The opening balance at 1 January in a business cash book was £673.42. During January payments totalled £6,419.37 and receipts totalled £6,488.20.

What is the closing balance on the cash book?

Activity 2

Below is a cash book that needs updating with the following receipts:

	£
10 May BACS	6,200
25 May Bank interest	40
31 May BACS	460

Enter the amounts into the cash book

Date	Details	£	Date	Chq	Details	£
1 May	Balance b/d	526	1 May			
6 May	Shaws	630	3 May	0041	Bills Farm	2,000
6 May	Andrew Ltd	880	3 May	0042	Cows Head	3,240
			5 May	0043	Adam Ant	840
			30 May	0044	Miles to Go	700

2 Preparing the bank reconciliation statement

2.1 Introduction

At regular intervals (normally at least once a month) the cashier must check that the cash book is correct by comparing the cash book with the bank statement.

2.2 Differences between the cash book and bank statement

At any date the balance shown on the bank statement is unlikely to agree with the balance in the cash book for two main reasons.

(a) **Items in the cash book not on the bank statement**

Certain items will have been entered in the cash book but will not appear on the bank statement at the time of the reconciliation. Examples are:

- Cheques received by the business and paid into the bank which have not yet appeared on the bank statement, due to the time lag of the clearing system. These are known as **outstanding lodgements** (can also be referred to as "uncleared lodgements").

- Cheques written by the business but which have not yet appeared on the bank statement, because the recipients have not yet paid them in, or the cheques are in the clearing system. These are known as **unpresented cheques**.

- Errors in the cash book (e.g. transposition of numbers, addition errors).

(b) **Items on the bank statement not in the cash book**

At the time of the bank reconciliation certain items will appear on the bank statement that have not yet been entered into the cash book. These can occur due to the cashier not being aware of the existence of these items until receiving the bank statements. Examples are:

- Direct debit or standing order payments that are in the bank statement but have not yet been entered in the cash payments book.

- BACS or other receipts paid directly into the bank account by a customer that have not yet been entered in the cash received book.

- Bank charges or bank interest that are unknown until the bank statement has been received and therefore will not be in the cash book.

- Errors in the cash book that may only come to light when the cash book entries are compared to the bank statement.

- Returned cheques i.e. cheques paid in from a customer who does not have sufficient funds in his bank to 'honour' the cheque (see later in this chapter).

2.3   The bank reconciliation

 Definition

A bank reconciliation is simply a statement that explains the differences between the balance in the cash book and the balance on the bank statement at a particular date.

A bank reconciliation is produced by following a standard set of steps.

Step 1:   Compare the cash book and the bank statement for the relevant period and identify any differences between them.

You should begin with agreeing the opening balances on the bank statement and cash book so that you are aware of any prior period reconciling items that exist.

This is usually done by ticking in the cash book and bank statement items that appear in both the cash book and the bank statement. Any items left unticked therefore only appear in one place, either the cash book or the bank statement. We saw in 2.2 above the reasons why this might occur.

Step 2:   Update the cash book for any items that appear on the bank statement that have not yet been entered into the cash book.

Tick these items in both the cash book and the bank statement once they are entered in the cash book.

At this stage there will be no unticked items on the bank statement.

(You clearly cannot enter on the bank statement items in the cash book that do not appear on the bank statement – the bank prepares the bank statement, not you. These items will either be unpresented cheques or outstanding lodgements – see 2.2 above.)

Step 3:   Bring down the new cash book balance following the adjustments in step 2 above.

Step 4: Prepare the bank reconciliation statement.

This will typically have the following layout:

Bank reconciliation as at 31.0X.200X

	£
Balance as per bank statement	X
Less unpresented cheques	(X)
Add outstanding lodgements	X
	___
Balance as per cash book	X
	___

Think for a moment to ensure you understand this layout.

We deduct the unpresented cheques (cheques already entered in the cash book but not yet on the bank statement) from the bank balance, because when they are paid into the bank the bank balance will be reduced.

We add outstanding lodgements (cash received and already entered in the cash book) because when they are paid into the bank they will increase the bank balance.

It is also useful to remember that the bank reconciliation can be performed by starting with the cash book balance and reconciling to the bank statement:

Bank reconciliation as at 31.0X.200X

	£
Balance as per cash book	X
Add unpresented cheques	(X)
Less outstanding lodgements	X
	___
Balance as per bank statement	X
	___

If we start with the cash book balance, to reconcile this to the bank statement balance we add back the unpresented cheques as though they haven't been paid out of the cash book (as the bank statement has not recognised these being paid out).

We deduct outstanding lodgements as though we haven't recognised these in the cash book (as the bank statement has not recognised these receipts). The cash book balance should then agree to the bank statement balance that is, we have reconciled these balances.

2.4 Debits and credits in bank statements

When comparing the cash book to the bank statement it is easy to get confused with debits and credits.

- When we pay money into the bank, we debit our cash book but the bank credits our account.

- This is because a debit in our cash book represents the increase in our asset 'cash'. For the bank, the situation is different: they will credit our account because they now owe us more money; in the bank's eyes we are a payable.

- When our account is overdrawn, we owe the bank money and consequently our cash book will show a credit balance. For the bank an overdraft is a debit balance.

On the bank statement a credit is an amount of money paid into the account and a debit represents a payment. A bank statement shows the transactions from the bank's point of view rather than the business' point of view.

 Example

On 30 April Tomasso's received the following bank statement as at 28 April.

Today's date is 30 April.

QC Bank
QC Street, London

To: Tomasso's   Account No 92836152   30 April 20x2

Date	Details	Payments	Receipts	Balance
20x2		£	£	£
2 April	Bal b/f			100
3 April	Cheque 101	55		45
4 April	Cheque 103	76		(31)
6 April	Bank Giro Credit		1,000	969
9 April	Cheque 105	43		926
10 April	Cheque 106	12		914
11 April	Cheque 107	98		816
21 April	Direct Debit RBC	100		716
22 April	Direct Debit OPO	150		566
23 April	Interest received		30	596
24 April	Bank charges	10		586
28 April	Bank Giro Credit DJA		250	836

The cash book at 28 April is shown below.

Date 20x2	Details	Bank £	Date 2012	Cheque number	Details	Bank £
	Balance b/f	100	01 April	101	Alan & Co	55
06 April	Prance Dance Co.	1,000	02 April	102	Amber's	99
23 April	Interest received	30	02 April	103	Kiki & Company	76
23 April	Graham Interiors	2,000	05 April	104	Marta	140
25 April	Italia Design	900	06 April	105	Nina Ltd	43
			07 April	106	Willy Wink	12
			08 April	107	Xylophones	98

Firstly, we see that the opening balance is £100 per both the bank statement and the cash book. Secondly, we must tick off the items in the bank statement to the cash book.

The effect of this on the bank statement can be seen below.

Date	Details	Payments £	Receipts £	Balance £
2 April	Bal b/f			100
3 April	Cheque 101	✔55		45
4 April	Cheque 103	✔76		(31)
6 April	Bank Giro Credit		✔1,000	969
9 April	Cheque 105	✔43		926
10 April	Cheque 106	✔12		914
11 April	Cheque 107	✔98		816
21 April	Direct Debit RBC	100		716
22 April	Direct Debit OPO	150		566
23 April	Interest received		✔30	596
24 April	Bank charges	10		586
28 April	Bank Giro Credit DJA		250	836

This leaves 4 items unticked on the bank statement. These transactions need to be added to the cash book and the cash book can then be balanced off.

The cash book is updated for these below:

Date 2012	Details	Bank £	Date 2012	Cheque number	Details	Bank £
	Balance b/d	100	01 April	101	Alan & Co	✓55
06 April	Prance Dance Co.	✓1,000	02 April	102	Amber's	99
23 April	Interest received	✓30	02 April	103	Kiki & Company	✓76
23 April	Graham Interiors	2,000	05 April	104	Marta	140
25 April	Italia Design	900	06 April	105	Nina Ltd	✓43
28 April	**DJA**	**250**	07 April	106	Willy Wink	✓12
			08 April	107	Xylophones	✓98
			21 April	–	**DD – RBC**	**100**
			22 April	–	**DD – OPO**	**150**
			24 April	–	**Bank charges**	**10**
			28 April	–	**Balance c/d**	3,497
		4,280				4,280
29 April	**Balance b/d**	**3,497**				

Once the cash book has been updated, there are 4 items unticked on the cash book.

These are the items that will go onto the bank reconciliation, as shown below.

Bank reconciliation statement as at 28 April	£
Balance per bank statement	836
Add:	
Name: Graham's Interior	2,000
Name: Italia Design	900
Total to add	2,900
Less:	
Name: Amber's	99
Name: Marta	140
Total to subtract	239
Balance as per cash book	3,497

The bank reconciliation statement proves that the difference between the balance on the bank statement and the balance on the cash book is due to outstanding lodgements and unpresented cheques.

Activity 3

FELICITY HOWE BOUTIQUE

Below is the cash book (bank columns only) of Felicity Howe Boutique for the month of April 20x4 together with her bank statement for the same period.

CASH BOOK

20x4		£	20X4		£
1 Apr	Balance b/d	1,470	2 Apr	Cheque 101129	930
9 Apr	Sales	606	4 Apr	Cheque 101130	506
12 Apr	Sales	1,048	9 Apr	Cheque 101131	834
30 Apr	Sales	550	29 Apr	Cheque 101132	410
			30 Apr	Balance c/d	994
		3,674			3,674
1 May	Balance b/d	994			

BANK STATEMENT

NORBURY BANK PLC
Southborough Branch
In account with: Felicity Howe   Account no 34578900

20X4		Payments	Receipts	Balance
01-Apr	balance b/f.			1,470
02-Apr	Cheque No. 129	930		540
05-Apr	Cheque No. 130	506		34
09-Apr	Counter Credit		606	640
12-Apr	Cheque No. 131	834		-194
12-Apr	Counter Credit		1,048	854
16-Apr	STO Hamble Comms.	75		779
17-Apr	BACS - Honey Bee		948	1,727
18-Apr	BACS - Goldfish CC	534		1,193
25-Apr	Overdraft fee		125	1,068
29-Apr	BGC S. May		610	1,678

Required:

a. Bring up to date the Cash Book making any adjustments necessary

b. Update the Cash Book and bring the balance down

c. Prepare a bank reconciliation statement as at 30 April 20x4

Activity 4

Graham

The cash book of Graham showed a debit balance of £204 on 31 March 20X3. A comparison with the bank statements revealed the following:

		£
1	Cheques drawn but not presented	3,168
2	Amounts paid into the bank but not credited	723
3	Entries in the bank statements not recorded in the cash account	
	(i) Standing orders	35
	(ii) Interest on bank deposit account	18
	(iii) Bank charges	14
4	Balance on the bank statement at 31 March	2,618

Tasks

a) Show the appropriate adjustments required in the cash book of Graham bringing down the correct balance at 31 March 20X3.

b) Prepare a bank reconciliation statement at that date.

 Activity 5

Below is a list of statements about bank reconciliations. Tick whether the statement is True or False.

Statement	True	False
Cheques take three (or more) days to clear		
An outstanding lodgement is a cheque that has been received by the business, paid into the bank, and has appeared on the bank statement		
An outstanding lodgement is a cheque that has been received by the business, paid into the bank, but has not yet appeared on the bank statement		
An unpresented cheque is one that has been written by the business but which has not yet appeared on the bank statement		
Direct debits that only show on the bank statement should be ignored		
Direct debits and standing orders that only show on the bank statement should be written into the cash book		
Bank charges are receipts to be entered into the cash book on the debit side		
Errors in the cash book may only come to light when the cash book entries are compared to the bank statement		

Answers to chapter activities

 Activity 1

	£
Opening balance	673.42
Payments	(6,419.37)
Receipts	6,488.20
Closing balance	742.25

The closing balance is £742.25 cash surplus.

 Activity 2

Updated cash book:

Date	Details	£	Date	Chq	Details	£
1 May	Balance b/d	526				
6 May	Shaws	630	3 May	0041	Bills Farm	2,000
6 May	Andrew Ltd	880	3 May	0042	Cows Head	3,240
10 May	BACS	6,200	5 May	0043	Adam Ant	840
25 May	Bank Interest	40	30 May	0044	Miles to Go	700
31 May	BACS	460				
			31 May		Balance c/d	1,956
		8,736				8,736
1 June	Balance b/d	1,956				

Activity 3

a. Bring up to date the Cash Book making any adjustments necessary

CASH BOOK

20x4		£	20x4		£
1 Apr	Balance b/d	1,470✓	2 Apr	Cheque 101129	930✓
9 Apr	Sales	606✓	4 Apr	Cheque 101130	506✓
12 Apr	Sales	1,048✓	9 Apr	Cheque 101131	834✓
30 Apr	Sales	550	29 Apr	Cheque 101132	410
			30 Apr	Balance c/d	994
		3,674			3,674
1 May	Balance b/d	994✓			

BANK STATEMENT

20x4		Payments	Receipts	Balance
01 Apr	Balance b/f			1,470✓
02 Apr	Cheque 101129	930✓		540
05 Apr	Cheque 101130	506✓		34
09 Apr	Counter credit		606✓	640
12 Apr	Cheque 101131	834✓		(194)
12 Apr	Counter credit		1,048✓	854
16 Apr	STO Hamble Comms	75✓		779
17 Apr	BACS – Honey Bee		948✓	1,727
18 Apr	BACS – Goldfish CC	534✓		1,193
25 Apr	Overdraft fee	125✓		1,068
29 Apr	BGC S May		610✓	1,678

b. Update the Cash Book and bring the balance down

FELICITY HOWE BOUTIQUE

CASH BOOK

20x4			20x4		
30 April	Balance b/d.	994.00✓			
				Hamble	
	Honey Bee	948.00✓	16 April	Comms.	75.00✓
	S. May	610.00✓	18 April	Goldfish CC	534.00✓
				Bank	
			25 April	charges	125.00✓
				Balance c/d.	1,818.00
		£ 2,552.00			£ 2,552.00
1 May	Balance b/d.	1,818.00			

c. Prepare a bank reconciliation statement as at 30 April 20x4

Felicity Howe Boutique **Bank reconciliation statement as at 30 April**	£
Balance per bank statement	1,678
Add:	
Name: Sales	550
Total to add	550
Less:	
Name: 101132	410
Total to subtract	410
Balance as per cash book	1,818

Activity 4

a)

Cash account

	£		£
Balance b/d	204	Sundry accounts	
Interest on deposit account	18	Standing orders	35
		Bank charges	14
		Balance c/d	173
	222		222
Balance b/d	173		

b)

BANK RECONCILIATION STATEMENT AT 31 MARCH 20X3

	£
Balance per bank statement	2,618
Add Outstanding lodgements	723
	3,341
Less Unpresented cheques	(3,168)
Balance per cash account	173

Activity 5

Statement	True	False
Cheques take three (or more) days to clear	✔	
An outstanding lodgement is a cheque that has been received by the business, paid into the bank, and has appeared on the bank statement		✔
An outstanding lodgement is a cheque that has been received by the business, paid into the bank, but has not yet appeared on the bank statement	✔	
An unpresented cheque is one that has been written by the business but which has not yet appeared on the bank statement	✔	
Direct debits that only show on the bank statement should be ignored		✔
Direct debits and standing orders that only show on the bank statement should be written into the cash book	✔	
Bank charges are receipts to be entered into the cash book on the debit side		✔
Errors in the cash book may only come to light when the cash book entries are compared to the bank statement	✔	

Spreadsheet Software

Introduction

Assessment of the unit is through a computer based project. Learners will be assessed against a set grid of marks that rewards them in line with the three learning outcomes identified below.

The following chapter provides full detail on all that students are required to do for this assessment including full coverage of the basics of setting up, formatting and using workbooks and worksheets. It also covers the Excel functions and calculations required for success at this level.

KNOWLEDGE
1 Use a spreadsheet to enter, edit and organise numerical and other data
2 Use appropriate formulas and tools to summarise spreadsheet information
3 Select and use appropriate tools and techniques to present spreadsheet information effectively

CONTENTS
1 Spreadsheet basics
2 Formatting worksheets
3 Simple calculations
4 Page presentation and printing
5 Excel functions
6 Assessment guidance

1 Spreadsheet basics

1.1 Spreadsheet Software Applications

There are many different spreadsheet applications available. Microsoft Excel is by far the most commonly used, and this Text is written for Microsoft Excel 2010.

1.2 Opening the application

There are numerous ways to open the application and the way that you do it will depend on the version of Excel that you are using and personal preference.

- Click the Windows button in the bottom left of the screen (or the Start Menu)
- Select (left click) 'All Programs'
- Select 'Microsoft Office'
- Select 'Microsoft Excel 2010'

From the bottom left hand corner of the screen:

Excel will open.

1.3 Workbooks and worksheets

Definition

A **worksheet** is a single page or sheet in the spreadsheet. A new spreadsheet will have 3 of these by default (called 'Sheet1', 'Sheet2', 'Sheet3'), but this can be changed, and worksheets can be added or deleted or renamed. The term worksheet is often abbreviated to **Sheet**.

A **workbook** is the spreadsheet file, made up of one or more worksheets. The default blank workbook is made up of 3 worksheets. The workbook name is the filename of the spreadsheet.

When Excel opens, a new, blank spreadsheet will be shown.

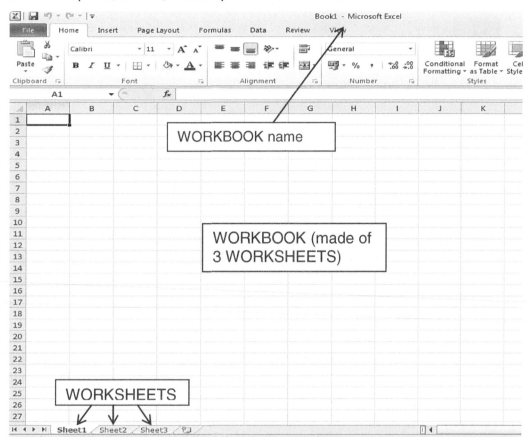

WORKBOOK name

WORKBOOK (made of 3 WORKSHEETS)

WORKSHEETS

1.4 The Ribbon

The 'Ribbon' is Excel's menu system. It is made up of various tabs and buttons, allowing you access to all of Excel's features. There are many, many options within the Ribbon – the good news is that most people only use a few of them. This guide will concentrate on the key features only.

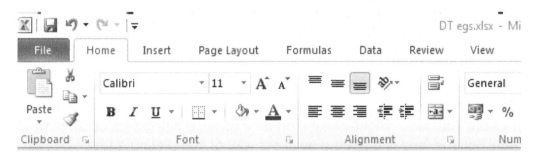

Tabs

There are usually 8 **tabs** across the top of the Ribbon – File, Home, Insert etc. and clicking on these offers different options. Sometimes more tabs appear depending on context – for example if you are editing a graph, the Chart Tools tabs appear.

Click on the name of the tab to change it, and see the different options.

This is the Insert Tab.

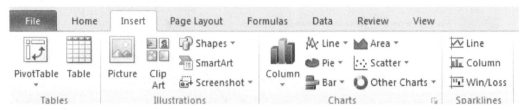

Buttons

The buttons on each tab perform a series of tasks – formatting, spreadsheet appearance, analysis etc. Some of them open up a new menu.

Many buttons have a small down arrow next to the name. Clicking on this opens brings up more options.

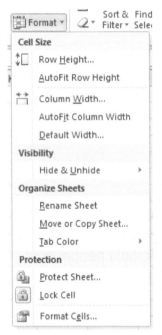

Although it seems like a lot to take in, the more you use these menu options, the more familiar with them you will become. Also, due to the way they are grouped with similar commands, you can often find what you need by looking in these menus.

Note that if you are not sure what a particular option does, hover the mouse pointer over it for a second or two and more information will be shown.

1.5 Right-click

Using the right mouse button within Excel (and most other Windows based programs) is very useful. Context-sensitive menus will appear depending on where you click. Right-clicking on an individual cell brings up several useful options, and is often the quickest way of completing a task.

1.6 Undo and Redo

Probably the most frequently used command within Excel. Undo, as the name suggests, cancels the last thing you did. The most useful thing about this is that it means you should not be afraid to experiment – if you are not sure what something does, try it. If it did not do what you wanted, undo.

Redo allows you to cancel an undo, if you decide that is what you did want!

The Undo button (the left arrow) is located in the top-left corner of the file. It is always visible, whichever tab you have clicked on in the ribbon.

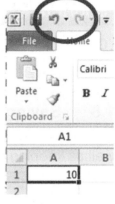

The Redo button (the right arrow) is greyed out as there are currently no commands to redo.

Clicking on the blue arrow will undo the last command. Clicking on the small triangle will allow you to undo more than one recent command.

After clicking Undo, the 10 which had been typed in has gone – this has been 'undone'. Note that the redo button has now turned blue – if we click on that, the command (typing 10 into cell A1) will be 'redone'.

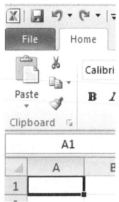

Remember, formatting, data entry and formula entry can all be 'undone', so if things start to look wrong, undo what you have done. If you realise you were right, simply redo!

Shortcut

- **Ctrl-z** (hold Ctrl, then press z) will undo the last command
- **Ctrl-y** will redo the last undone command

1.7 Opening a new workbook

If you wish to open a new workbook:

- Select the **File** tab
- Select '**New**'
- Select '**Blank workbook**' from Available Templates.

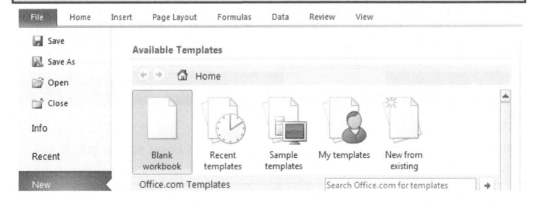

Shortcut

Ctrl-n

Opens a new workbook automatically.

1.8   Saving the workbook

Saving the workbook allows you to give it a more appropriate name, as well as keeping it for future use. To save a file:

- Select the File tab
- Select Save to save the file as it is, or Save As to give it a new name
- The 'Save As' Dialogue Box will open. Navigate to the directory in which you wish to save the file
- Type the name of the spreadsheet in the File name box
- Click 'Save'.

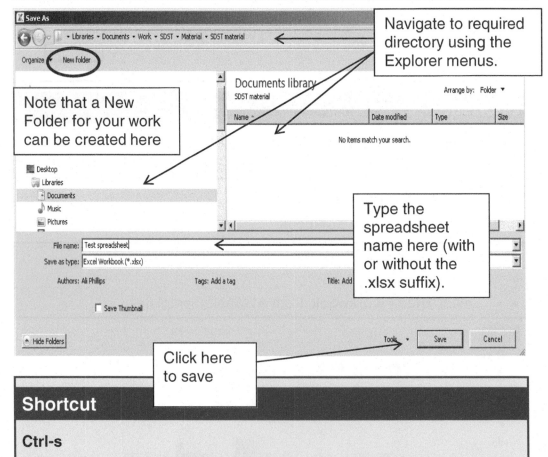

Navigate to required directory using the Explorer menus.

Note that a New Folder for your work can be created here

Type the spreadsheet name here (with or without the .xlsx suffix).

Click here to save

Shortcut

Ctrl-s

Will reveal the 'Save' dialogue box if a file hasn't been saved yet. It will save a file that already has a name.

1.9 Opening an existing workbook

To work on a spreadsheet that has been previously saved, open Excel as before, then:

- Click the 'File' tab in the top left of the screen
- Click the 'Open' button
- Navigate to the file you wish to open
- Click the 'Open' button, or double click on the file.

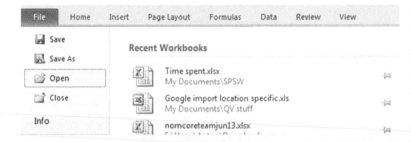

Notice that recently used workbooks can also be selected without having to use the 'Open' button.

Shortcut

Ctrl-o

Will reveal the 'Open' dialogue box.

1.10 Closing the workbook

Having saved your workbook you can then close it. There are 2 options:

1 Click the 'X' in the top right hand corner of the screen – the lower one of the two (the top one closes Excel completely). If you have multiple worksheets open then you get the option to close just the one you are working on.

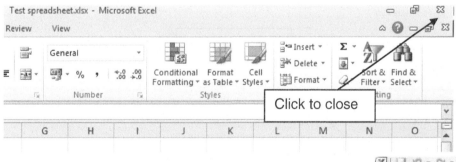

2 Select the File tab, and then Close.

If you haven't already saved the workbook you will be prompted to do so when you click 'Close'. You can then follow the procedure above.

1.11 Renaming the workbook

To 'Rename' your workbook you could:

(a) Save the file using a different name, using Save As (note that this will keep a copy of the original file)

(b) Or with the workbook closed

- Locate the File using Windows Explorer (or My Computer)
- Right Click on the file and select 'Rename'
- Type the new name
- Press Enter.

Shortcut

F2
Renames a file in Windows Explorer.

Shortcut

On your keyboard you have a key with the 'Windows' icon
Press '**Windows-e**' to open Windows Explorer.

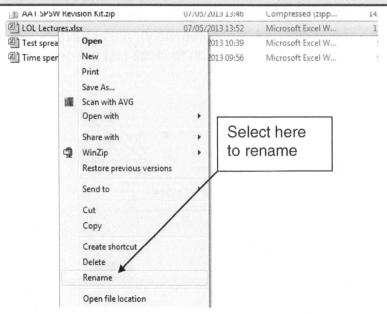

Select here to rename

1.12 Renaming a worksheet

To 'Rename' a particular **worksheet** within a **workbook** you should do the following:

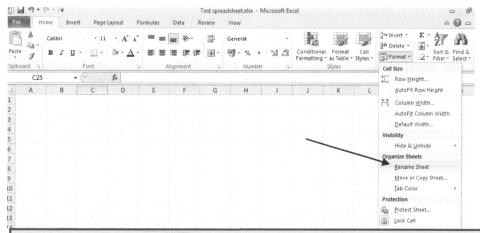

- Select the Home tab
- Select Format
- Select Rename Sheet
- The Sheet name will then be highlighted. Type the new name to overwrite it.

OR

- Right click on the worksheet name at the bottom of the page
- Select rename
- The Sheet name will then be highlighted. Type the new name to overwrite it.

Or

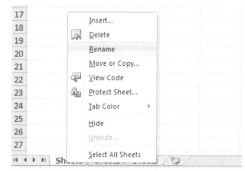

The quickest way is just to **DOUBLE CLICK** on the sheet name to edit it.

1.13 Adding worksheets

There are two ways to achieve this, as with renaming a worksheet:

- Select the Home tab
- Select Insert
- Select Insert Sheet
- A new sheet will be added

OR

* Right click on the worksheet name at the bottom of the page
* Select Insert
* Select Worksheet
* A new sheet will be added

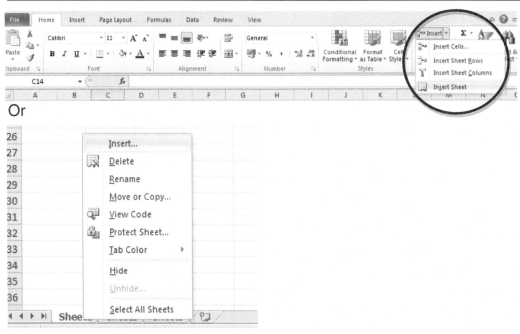

Or

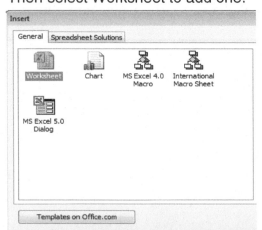

Then select Worksheet to add one.

Shortcut

Shift+F11
Inserts a new worksheet

1.14 Deleting worksheets

Similar method to adding worksheets:

- Select the Home tab
- Select Delete
- Select Delete Sheet
- A warning will show – click Delete
- The current sheet will be deleted.

OR

- Right click on the worksheet name at the bottom of the page
- Select Delete
- A warning will show – click Delete
- The current sheet will be deleted.

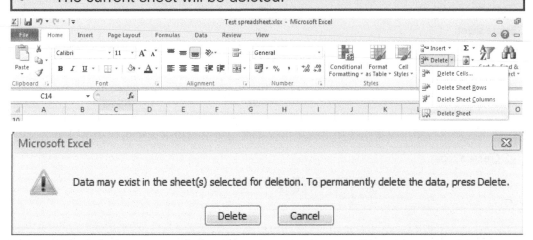

Warning message – take note, once a sheet has been deleted this action **CANNOT** be undone.

1.15 Moving/Copying worksheets

The order of your worksheets can easily be changed in Excel, and you can also quickly copy a sheet to get a duplicate version.

- Select Format on the Home tab
- Select Move or Copy Sheet
- A Dialogue box will open – select where you want the current sheet to be located
- Click OK when complete.

OR

- Right click on the worksheet name at the bottom of the page
- Select Move or Copy
- The same dialogue box will be displayed.

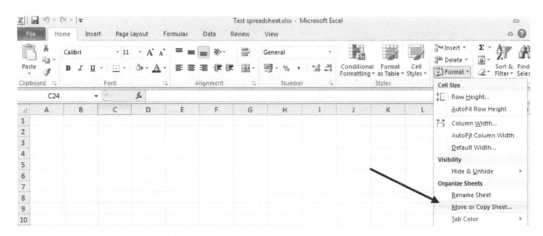

Shortcut

Simply **LEFT CLICK** and **HOLD** the button down while pointing at the sheet name – then **DRAG** the sheet to the position you require

Note that a worksheet can be moved within the existing workbook, or to another workbook you have open. To copy a worksheet, follow exactly the same steps, but tick the 'Create a copy' box before clicking OK.

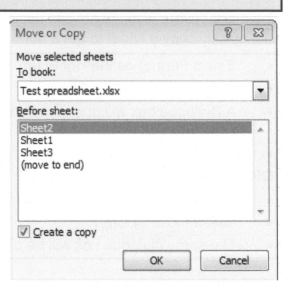

Shortcut

If using the **LEFT-CLICK** and **DRAG** approach above, hold down **Ctrl** before releasing the mouse button. A + will appear by the mouse pointer, and a copy made of the worksheet.

1.16 Spreadsheet structure

The spreadsheet (worksheet) shown above is made up of 'Rows', 'Columns' and 'Cells:

- The 'Rows' are numbered down the left hand-side from 1 onwards.
- The 'Columns' are lettered along the top from A onwards.
- The 'Cells' are the junction of columns and rows [example cell A1 is the junction of Column A and Row 1].
- The 'Active' cell is where you are be able to enter data and is highlighted with a bold border [See B4 above]. Both the column letter and the row number are also highlighted.

Shortcut

Ctrl-Home takes you to cell A1.

Ctrl-End takes you to the cell furthest into the worksheet that has been active (even if the content has been removed).

1.17 Entering data into your worksheet

Selecting cells

To select a cell, left-click on the cell you wish to select. This is now the Active Cell. The value or formula in the Active Cell will be shown in the Formula Bar, and the Cell Reference will be shown in the Name Box.

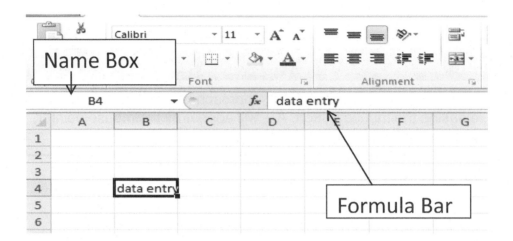

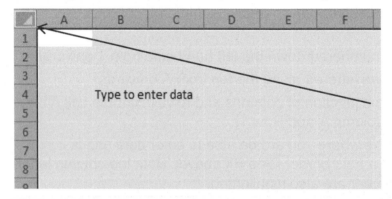

You can also change the selection by using the arrow keys to move the Active Cell Box around the screen until you reach the cell you require, or by typing the cell you require into the Name Box and pressing 'Enter'.

Selecting multiple cells

Selecting several cells at once is easiest using the mouse.

- Using the mouse, **Left-Click** on a cell to select it, but **HOLD DOWN** the mouse button
- **DRAG** the mouse pointer to select neighbouring cells.

If you wish to select non-contiguous (not neighbouring) cells, press the Ctrl key while selecting individual cells.

To select **ALL** cells in a worksheet, click on the box in the top-left of the sheet.

Cell ranges

As we have seen, each cell in Excel has a name (A1, B7 etc). If you select multiple cells, this is a **RANGE** of cells. If you select 2 separate cells, for example C2 and E5, the cells would be separated by a comma, so this would be displayed as **(C2, E5)**. If, as is more common, a **BLOCK** of cells is selected, these are displayed as:

(Top left cell:Bottom right cell)

For example:

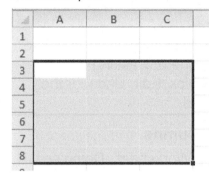

To refer to the cells selected, we would enter **(A3:C8)**.

This notation becomes important when we deal with functions later.

Entering data

To enter data into the active cell, simply type the data required into the cell – either numeric or text. This will overwrite any existing data.

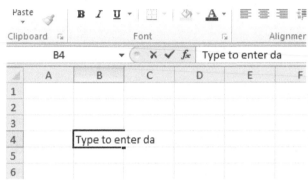

As you type, the data will be displayed on the spreadsheet itself and within the Formula Bar.

1.18   Editing and deleting cell content

Editing existing data

If a cell already contains data and you wish to edit it without overwriting, there are two ways to do this, via the Formula Bar or directly in the cell:

- **Double Click** on a cell to edit it

Or

- With the cell selected, **Left-click** in the **Formula Bar** to edit its contents.

Shortcut

Press **F2** to edit the Active cell

Deleting data

To **delete** cell content you can do the following

1   Go to the cell you wish to delete. Press the delete key. You can highlight multiple cells and delete in the same way.

2   'Right-Click' in the active cell and then 'Left-Click' **clear contents.** You can highlight multiple adjacent cells and delete in the same way.

CAUTION!!!

If you 'Right-Click' and then click 'delete' Excel thinks you want to delete the cells completely. You will be offered a dialogue box asking you which way you want to shift the cells. You can click 'Edit, Undo' or the undo icon on the toolbar if you change your mind.

1.19 Inserting and deleting rows and columns

You can insert both rows and columns into your 'Worksheet'. Doing so will not increase or decrease the number of rows and columns in your worksheet. Excel will merely insert a blank row(s) or column(s) and shift the other rows or columns down/right. Excel cannot insert if the last row or column are in use. You would need to delete a row or column from elsewhere first.

To add a row to your worksheet

- Select the **'Home'** tab
- Select **'Insert'**
- Select **'Insert Sheet Rows'**

A row will be inserted, and the row with the Active Cell in it will be shifted **DOWN**.

To add a column to your worksheet

- Select the **'Home'** tab
- Select **'Insert'**
- Select **'Insert Sheet Columns'**

A column will be inserted, and the column with the Active Cell in it will be shifted **RIGHT**.

Shortcut

'Right-Click' the row number or column letter where you wish to insert, then click **'Insert'**

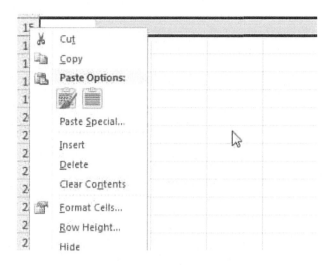

Right clicking on the '**15**' brings up this menu – select Insert to insert a row here.

To delete a row from your worksheet

- Select the '**Home**' tab
- Select '**Delete**'
- Select '**Delete Sheet Rows**'

The data in the row will be deleted, and the rows underneath shifted **UP**

To delete a column from your worksheet

- Select the '**Home**' tab
- Select '**Delete**'
- Select '**Delete Sheet Columns**'

The data in the column will be deleted, and the columns underneath shifted **UP**

Shortcut

'Right-Click' the row number(s) or column letter(s) you wish to delete, then click '**Delete**'

1.20 Copy, Cut, Paste and AutoFill

Copy and paste

Excel allows you to copy data from the 'Active Cell(s)' to other cells.

- Click in the active cell(s)
- Select the **'Home'** tab
- Press the **'Copy'** button
- Select the cell (or cells) where you wish to copy to
- Press the **'Paste'** button

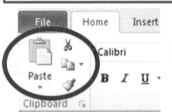 Copy and paste are together on the Ribbon

Shortcut

'**Right-Click**' the 'Active Cell(s)'. Click '**Copy**'.

Select the cell(s) where you wish to copy to.

'**Right-Click**' and then click '**Paste**'.

Shortcut

Highlight the active cells.

Ctrl-c will copy the selected cell(s)

Ctrl-v will paste the copied cell(s) to the location you have selected

Cut and paste

Excel allows you to move data from the 'Active Cell(s)' to other cells.

- Click in the active cell(s)
- Select the **'Home'** tab
- Press the **'Cut'** button
- Select the cell (or cells) where you wish to move to
- Press the **'Paste'** button

Shortcut

'**Right-Click**' the 'Active Cell(s)'. Click '**Cut**'.

Select the cell(s) where you wish to copy to.

'**Right-Click**' and then click '**Paste**'.

Shortcut
Highlight the active cells. **Ctrl-x** will copy the selected cell(s) **Ctrl-v** will paste the copied cell(s) to the location you have selected

AutoFill

The AutoFill tool is an incredibly useful feature within Excel. In the main it is used to quickly copy data into neighbouring cells, but it has several other uses that can save time and effort.

To copy a cell's contents into adjacent cells, hover the mouse pointer over the **bottom right** of the cell. The mouse pointer should change from a fat cross (⊕) to a normal cross.

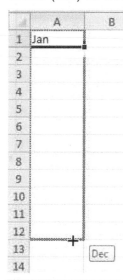

Once the pointer has changed as shown, **left click** and **drag** the mouse in the direction you wish to copy the information.

Release the mouse button to complete the fill.

Autofill becomes especially useful when copying formulas (see later), and can also be used to save time when typing out common lists, such as days of the week, or repetitive sequences.

Here, 'Jan' has been typed into cell A1. Autofill has been used to 'drag' the cell down for 12 rows. You can see a pop up over B13 there's a box saying 'Dec' – this is telling us that the Autofill is going to put 'Dec' in cell A12 – the last cell in the fill.

The Autofill is complete. Note that if cell A1 was 'January', the other cells would be populated with the full month name too.

Days of the week are another common autofill.

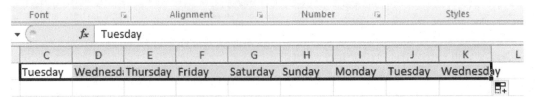

You can also autofill sequences of numbers. To do this you need to have at least the first 2 numbers of the sequence. Highlight both cells and then 'drag' the cells down.

AutoFill completes the sequence.

1.21 Paste Special

There is another function 'Paste Special'. This allows you to paste different aspects of what could be contained in a cell.

* **Copy** the cell(s) you wish to Paste
* **Select** the destination cell(s)
* **Left-click** the down arrow underneath the **Paste** button on the **Home** tab
* Select **Paste Special**

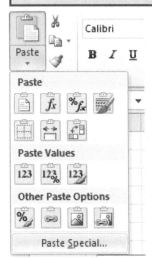

Here you can either select Paste Special, or one of the buttons shown to paste certain features only. Hover over each button to see what they do – a very commonly used one in Paste Values, which removes any formulas and just pastes the cell values.

Shortcut

Ctrl-c to copy the cells
Ctrl-Alt-v to paste special

The Paste Special menu gives all of the options available:

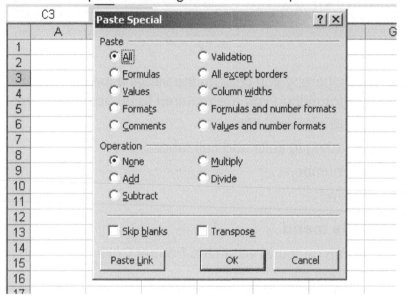

(i)   **'All'** pastes content, formula and formatting but it will not alter column width.

(ii)   **'Formulas'** pastes the formula from the cell(s) to the new location, without affecting the formatting of the destination cell.

(iii)   **'Values'** pastes the value of a cell and not the formula that may have created the value.

(iv)   **'Formats'** pastes any formatting that you might have carried out to the new cell(s). This includes cell shading, borders and number formats, but not column width.

(v)   **'Comments'** pastes any comments that have been entered into a cell to the new location. '**Comments**' allow you to write a note about a particular cell for you – and others – to see.

Once you have written your comment you will be able to delete and/or hide it by 'Right-Clicking' again in the 'Active Cell'.

You will also note that part of the 'Paste-Special' dialogue box allows you to carry out operations. For example the **'add'** operation will add the value of the 'Active Cell' to the value of the cell(s) that you are pasting to. It will add formula outcomes to values and it will also add formulas to formulas.

The last part of the 'Paste-Special' dialogue box allows two other actions

(i)   **'Skip Blanks'** ignores the content –formatting etc – of a cell with no data in it. However, it does maintain the gaps between non-adjacent cells.

(ii) **'Transpose'** is a useful tool for pasting the content of a column into a row, and vice-versa.

2 Formatting worksheets

2.1 Introduction

Formatting is a process whereby you change the visual aspects of your worksheet. The types of formatting you are required to be able to do are:

1   Adjust row height and column width.

2   Add borders and shading to cells and cell ranges.

3   Formatting text and numbers.

4   Hide columns and rows.

2.2 The format cells menu

Most formatting options can be found within the Format Cells menu. To view the Format Cells menu:

> - Select the cell(s) you wish to format
> - In the **Home** menu, select **Format Cells**
>
> **OR**
>
> - **Right-Click** on the cell(s) to format
> - Select Format Cells

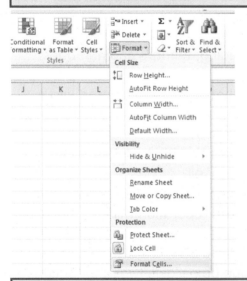

Shortcut

Press **Ctrl-1** to bring up the format cells menu.

The **Format Cells** menu has several options, as summarised below:

Number	Changes number formats, for example the number of decimal places, currency type or percentages.
Alignment	Allows adjustment of where data is shown within a cell for example left or right alignment, and merging cells together.
Font	Appearance and size of text, along with special features like bold and underline.
Border	Affects the cell itself, rather than the data within – place lines of varying size and colours around the cell.
Fill	Colour the cell in various shades and patterns.
Protection	Affects whether a cell can be edited (dealt with later).

To Exit the menu, click OK to accept changes, or Cancel to reject them.

2.3 Number formats

Although the name implies that this affects numbers, this option will change the way information within all selected cells will be displayed. Its primary use is to display numeric information in a user-friendly fashion.

General

The default format is 'General', where no special formatting will apply.

50
15.6
1005
-516
text
text and 2432

This sample data shows how Excel displays numbers and text by default – with no special formatting.

Number

This format gives more options on how to display numbers. The options are number of decimal places, whether to separate thousands with a comma, and how to display negative numbers:

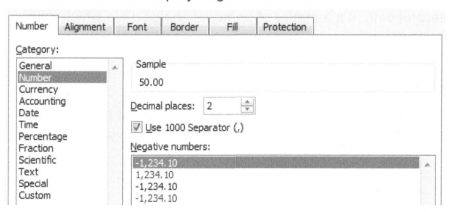

The Sample window shows what the cell will look like with the current options selected. The 1000 separator is an excellent way of making numeric data easier to read. The negative number option can be used to display negative numbers as red, with or without a minus sign.

50.00
15.60
1,005.00
-516.00
text
text and 2432

The same information now formatted as a Number. Note that the text information in the bottom two cells is unchanged – even though there is a number in the final cell, Excel recognises it as text only, and will not format the number separately (this can be done, but is beyond the scope of the syllabus).

Currency

This is very similar to **Number**, with the added option of putting a currency symbol at the front of the number:

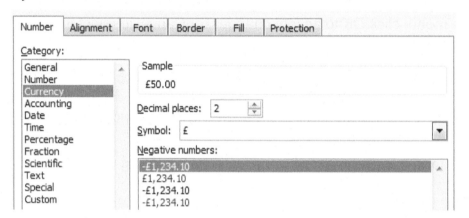

£50.00
£15.60
£1,005.00
-£516.00
text
text and 2432

The only difference is the "£" sign at the front of the numbers.

Accounting

This is very similar to **Currency**, but decimal points and currency symbols will be lined up in a column, potentially making it easier to interpret data. It's a matter of personal choice as to which you prefer.

Percentage

This enables numbers to be displayed with a '%' symbol at the end, and also multiplies the value in the cell by 100 – this will be covered in more detail later.

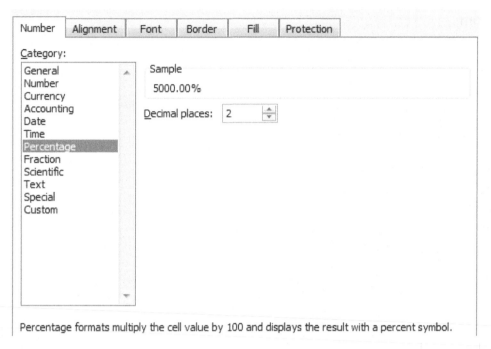

If 0.1 is typed in a cell and percentage formatting is applied then this will be changed to 10%. 0.5 will be changed to 50%. The % format will come in very useful later on.

0.1	
10%	
0.5	
50%	

Date

The **Date** format is used to display dates in various different ways. The best thing to do is type the date in you wish to use, and then select the different options until you find the one you want:

If you type something that looks like a date into Excel, it will convert it to the default date format once Enter is pressed.

23-11-78

Default format is dd/mm/yyyy   23/11/1978

Choosing the appropriate option will display the date as required.

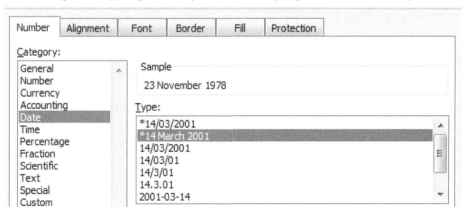

Custom

In the **custom** number list there are a number of formats that can be adapted to create the formatting required.

In the option highlighted above -2345.68 would be (in red):   -2,346

#,##0;[Red]-#,##0, formats numbers to have no decimal places and negative numbers shown in red with a minus sign in front.

You can change this to use brackets instead of the minus sign:

Type:

#,##0;[Red]-#,##0

General

The value now looks like: (2,346)

You can also change the colour if required to Black, Green, White, Blue, Magenta, Yellow, or Cyan or keep it as Red, by changing the word in square brackets [ ].

It is possible to use custom number formats to actually hide the content of a cell[s]. For example in the sheet below you can see the salaries of Directors P, Q and R. For the sake of confidentiality it might be considered best to hide individual figures but keep the total visible.

This can be achieved by highlighting the figures you want to hide and then creating the custom number format as below to hide the content.

Three semi-colons ;;; followed by OK will hide the contents of cells

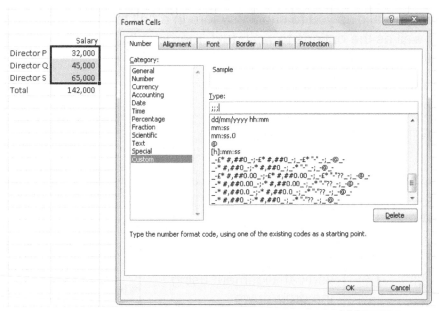

The individual salaries are now hidden from view on the worksheet but if the individual cells are clicked into the values still show in the formula bar.

Shortcuts

There are several shortcuts available to change the Number Format on the **Home menu**.

Number formats can be chosen directly, or percentage symbols, 1000 separators and number of decimal points changed.

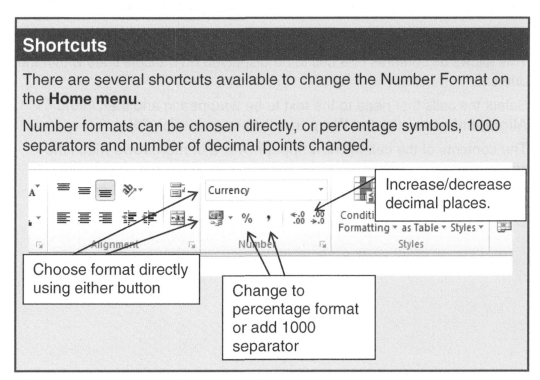

2.4 Alignment

The **Alignment** tab allows you to choose where in a cell text will be displayed, as well as the options to wrap text, merge cells, shrink text to fit in cells and also adjust orientation of the text in a cell.

Text alignment

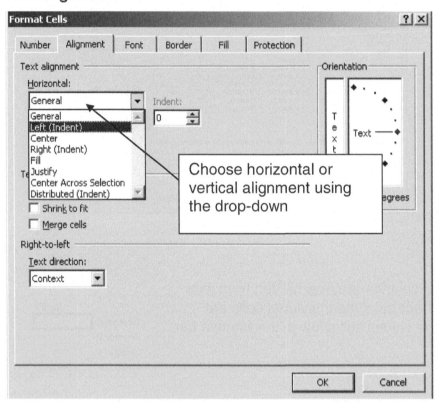

Wrap text

This allows all contents of a cell to be displayed on multiple lines within the one cell.

Select the cells that need to the text to be wrapped in and then in the **Alignment** menu, tick the **Wrap text** tickbox, and click **OK**.

The contents of the cell will now appear over 2 or more rows within the single cell.

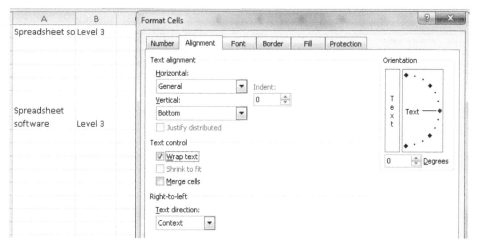

Shrink to fit

An alternative to wrapping the text is to decrease the size of the text to fit in the cell. Again select the cell that needs adjusting and click in the **Shrink to fit** tickbox and click **OK**.

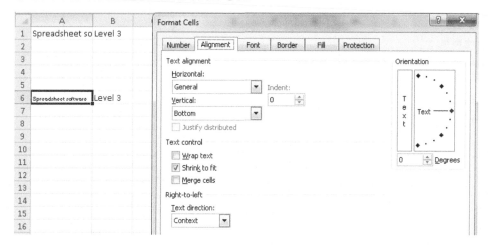

Merge cells

Merging cells joins them together so Excel treats them as one cell. This can be useful for headings that run over more than one column, for example, or if you wish to create a heading across a whole page.

	A	B	C	D	E	F	G	H	I	J	K	L	M	N
1	Monthly Profit Calculations													
2		January	February	March	April	May	June	July	August	Septembe	October	Novembe	December	
3	Sales	10,000	12,500	11,000	12,200	12,500	13,000	11,000	16,000	15,000	15,500	12,000	10,200	
4	Costs	6,500	7,000	7,000	6,700	7,200	8,000	7,500	8,200	6,800	7,100	5,500	5,200	
5	Profit	3,500	5,500	4,000	5,500	5,300	5,000	3,500	7,800	8,200	8,400	6,500	5,000	
6														

The heading for this data would look nicer if it was centred across the columns. This can be done firstly by merging the cells, then by centering.

First, **select** the **cells** you wish to merge:

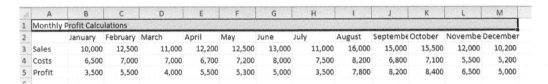

	A	B	C	D	E	F	G	H	I	J	K	L	M
1	Monthly Profit Calculations												
2		January	February	March	April	May	June	July	August	Septembe	October	Novembe	December
3	Sales	10,000	12,500	11,000	12,200	12,500	13,000	11,000	16,000	15,000	15,500	12,000	10,200
4	Costs	6,500	7,000	7,000	6,700	7,200	8,000	7,500	8,200	6,800	7,100	5,500	5,200
5	Profit	3,500	5,500	4,000	5,500	5,300	5,000	3,500	7,800	8,200	8,400	6,500	5,000

In the **Alignment** menu, tick the **Merge Cells** tickbox, and click **OK**. The cells will now be treated as one big cell.

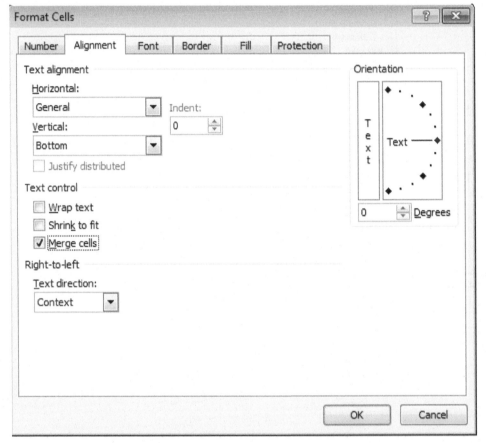

	A	B	C	D	E	F	G	H	I	J	K	L	M
1	Monthly Profit Calculations												
2		January	February	March	April	May	June	July	August	Septembe	October	Novembe	December
3	Sales	10,000	12,500	11,000	12,200	12,500	13,000	11,000	16,000	15,000	15,500	12,000	10,200
4	Costs	6,500	7,000	7,000	6,700	7,200	8,000	7,500	8,200	6,800	7,100	5,500	5,200
5	Profit	3,500	5,500	4,000	5,500	5,300	5,000	3,500	7,800	8,200	8,400	6,500	5,000
6													

In the Alignment menu then select **Horizontal Alignment** as **Center** to show your heading in the centre of the data.

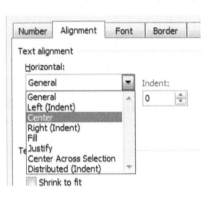

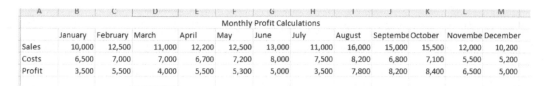

	January	February	March	April	May	June	July	August	Septembe	October	Novembe	December
					Monthly Profit Calculations							
Sales	10,000	12,500	11,000	12,200	12,500	13,000	11,000	16,000	15,000	15,500	12,000	10,200
Costs	6,500	7,000	7,000	6,700	7,200	8,000	7,500	8,200	6,800	7,100	5,500	5,200
Profit	3,500	5,500	4,000	5,500	5,300	5,000	3,500	7,800	8,200	8,400	6,500	5,000

Orientation

Using orientation allows you to rotate the text in a cell to a diagonal angle or vertical orientation. This is often useful for labelling columns that are narrow.

As with the other alignment formatting, highlight the text that needs the orientation changed and choose the degree of angle you require:

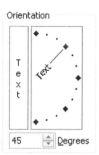

Shortcuts

Home tab, alignment section:

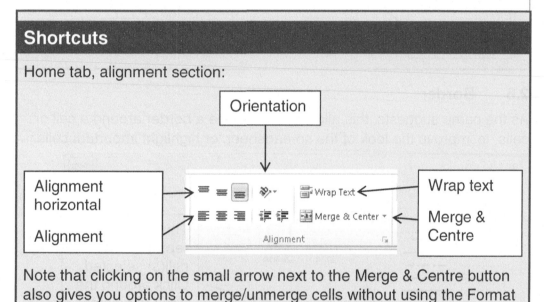

Note that clicking on the small arrow next to the Merge & Centre button also gives you options to merge/unmerge cells without using the Format Cells menu.

2.5 Font

This is used to change the font type, size, and colour and to add effects to the text – the options are fairly self-explanatory:

Shortcuts

The Font options can also be selected from the font section of the **Home Menu.**

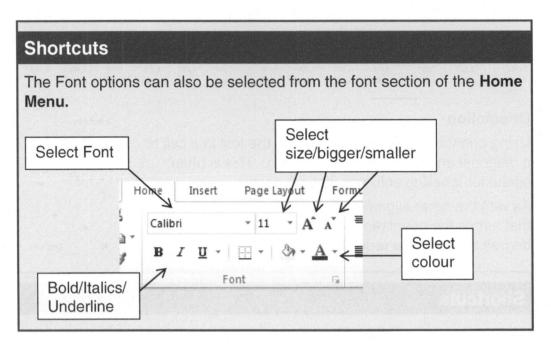

Select Font

Select size/bigger/smaller

Select colour

Bold/Italics/Underline

2.6 Border

As the name suggests, this allows you to place a border around a cell or cells, to improve the look of the spreadsheet, or highlight important cells.

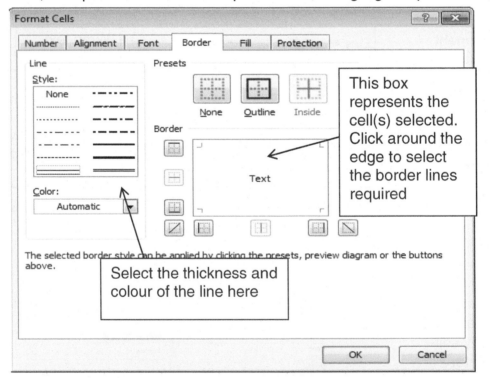

This box represents the cell(s) selected. Click around the edge to select the border lines required

Select the thickness and colour of the line here

If several cells are selected, the same borders will be applied to each:

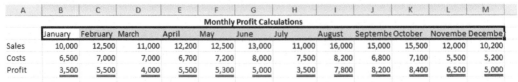

	A	B	C	D	E	F	G	H	I	J	K	L	M
						Monthly Profit Calculations							
		January	February	March	April	May	June	July	August	Septembe	October	Novembe	Decembe
Sales		10,000	12,500	11,000	12,200	12,500	13,000	11,000	16,000	15,000	15,500	12,000	10,200
Costs		6,500	7,000	7,000	6,700	7,200	8,000	7,500	8,200	6,800	7,100	5,500	5,200
Profit		3,500	5,500	4,000	5,500	5,300	5,000	3,500	7,800	8,200	8,400	6,500	5,000

KAPLAN PUBLISHING

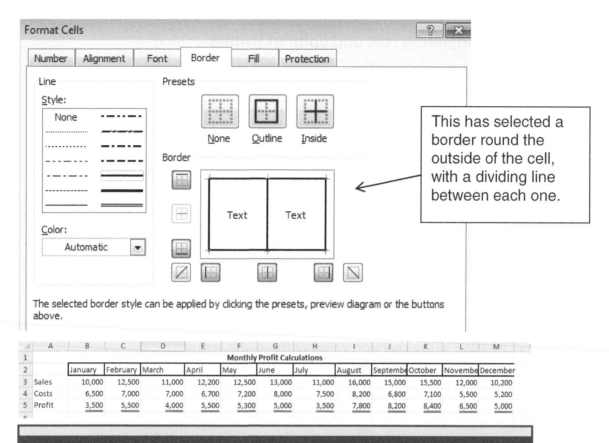

A	B	C	D	E	F	G	H	I	J	K	L	M
1					Monthly Profit Calculations							
2	January	February	March	April	May	June	July	August	September	October	November	December
3 Sales	10,000	12,500	11,000	12,200	12,500	13,000	11,000	16,000	15,000	15,500	12,000	10,200
4 Costs	6,500	7,000	7,000	6,700	7,200	8,000	7,500	8,200	6,800	7,100	5,500	5,200
5 Profit	3,500	5,500	4,000	5,500	5,300	5,000	3,500	7,800	8,200	8,400	6,500	5,000

Shortcut

Borders can be applied directly using the **borders** button in the **Home Menu**

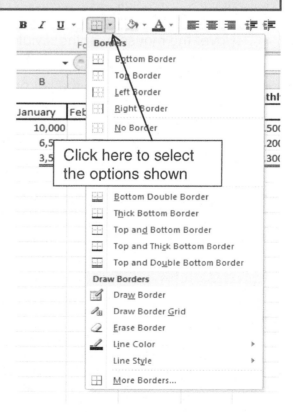

The appropriate border can be selected directly from here.

2.7 Adjusting row and column widths

Adjusting column width

You may need to adjust column widths so that all of your data is shown. For example in the screenshot below, columns J, L and M are not wide enough to display the month properly.

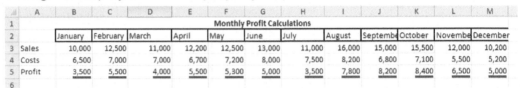

	A	B	C	D	E	F	G	H	I	J	K	L	M
1						Monthly Profit Calculations							
2		January	February	March	April	May	June	July	August	Septembe	October	Novembe	December
3	Sales	10,000	12,500	11,000	12,200	12,500	13,000	11,000	16,000	15,000	15,500	12,000	10,200
4	Costs	6,500	7,000	7,000	6,700	7,200	8,000	7,500	8,200	6,800	7,100	5,500	5,200
5	Profit	3,500	5,500	4,000	5,500	5,300	5,000	3,500	7,800	8,200	8,400	6,500	5,000
6													

There are several ways to adjust the column width.

- Select the Column or Columns you wish to change the width of
- In the '**Home Menu'**, select **Format** (in the **Cells** section)
- Select Column Width
- Type in the numeric value of the width required.

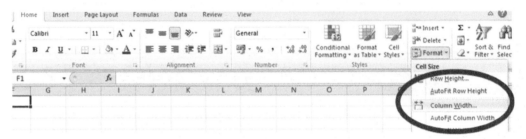

Alternatively (and usually easier), adjust the columns visually as follows:

- Hover the mouse over the dividing line between two columns. The mouse pointer will change to ⊹
- **Left click** and **drag** to the left or right to adjust the width as required
- Release the mouse button to accept the new width.

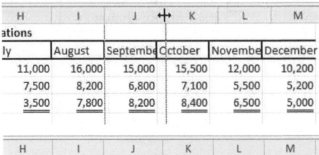

H	I	J	K	L	M
ations					
ly	August	Septembe	October	Novembe	December
11,000	16,000	15,000	15,500	12,000	10,200
7,500	8,200	6,800	7,100	5,500	5,200
3,500	7,800	8,200	8,400	6,500	5,000

Drag the mouse to the left or right to adjust the column width.

H	I	J	K	L	M
lations					
ıly	August	September	October	Novembe	December
11,000	16,000	15,000	15,500	12,000	10,200
7,500	8,200	6,800	7,100	5,500	5,200
3,500	7,800	8,200	8,400	6,500	5,000

Once the mouse button is released, the column will be the correct width.

Adjusting row height

This works in exactly the same way as adjusting column widths.

- Select the Row or Rows you wish to change the height of
- In the **'Home Menu'**, select **Format** (in the **Cells** section)
- Select Row Height
- Type in the numeric value of the width required.

Or

- Hover the mouse over the dividing line between two rows. The mouse pointer will change to +
- **Left click** and **drag** up or down to adjust the height as required
- Release the mouse button to accept the new height.

2.8 Autofit

A very useful feature for setting column widths/row heights is **Autofit**. You may have seen this option when selecting a column width:

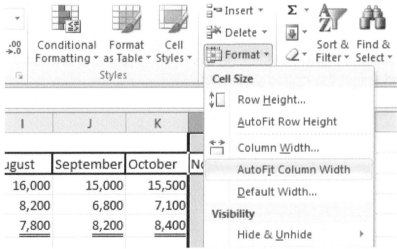

Selecting Autofit will set the column width or row height to match the largest cell in the column. This way you know that all of your data will be visible.

Shortcut

Hover the mouse pointer over the dividing line between two columns/rows and **DOUBLE CLICK** to autofit.

Autofit all rows/columns

After your work is finished, it is sensible to Autofit all rows/columns to ensure that everything is visible.

This is quickly and easily achieved as follows:

> - Click the **Select All Cells** button in the top left of the spreadsheet
> - Autofit **ANY** column
> - Autofit **Any** row
>
> All columns and rows will be correctly adjusted.

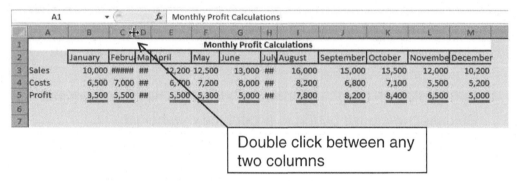

Double click between any two columns

All columns are now wide enough to display their data.

2.9 Hide and unhide columns and rows

It is possible to hide columns or rows on a worksheet. Select the column(s) or row(s) that need to be hidden and on the **Home** tab in the **Cells** section you will find **Format**. Click on the down arrow and choose **Hide & unhide** and select the option you want.

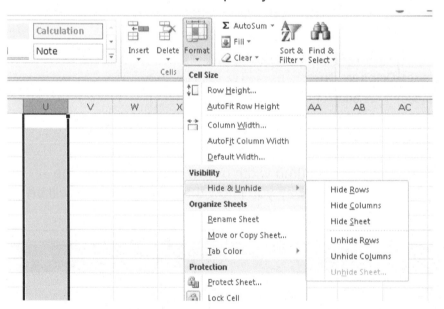

You can see if a column or row is hidden as the letter or number representing the column or row is missing.

Column U is hidden in this example:

.

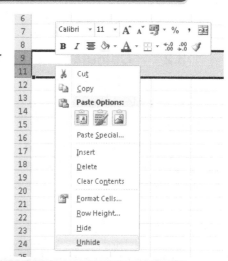

To unhide a row or column highlight the rows or columns on either side of the hidden row or column, right click on the mouse and choose unhide.

You can also unhide by using the Cells section on the home tab and Format.

3 Simple calculations

3.1 Simple calculations

We have already seen how to enter numeric and text information into cells. However, Excel's primary purpose is to manipulate the raw data through calculations and formulas. One of the main things you will use Excel for is simple calculations. The most basic (and most common) calculations are the mathematical functions addition +, subtraction -, multiplication * and divide /.

To use these, you need to tell Excel that you are using a **FUNCTION**. To do this, enter an equals sign, '=', before the calculation you require.

So, to find the answer to 3+5, type in any cell   **=3+5** and press **Enter**.

As you type, the formula is displayed above, in the formula bar, as well as on the spreadsheet itself.

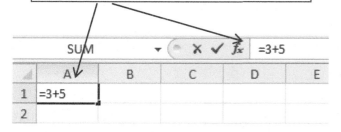

Once enter is pressed, the result of the calculation is shown on the spreadsheet, but the calculation itself is still shown in the formula bar.

Excel can be used in this way as a simple calculator by entering the calculation required, using +, -, * or /.

3.2   Calculations using existing values

Excel is particularly useful when using the values in other cells as part of your calculations. Take the following example:

	A	B	C	D
1	Name	Hourly Rate	Hours Worked	Pay
2	Srnicek	£8.60	30	
3	Watson	£8.60	20	
4	Peacock	£9.00	20	
5	Albert	£11.50	25	
6	Beresford	£10.50	30	
7	Batty	£12.00	40	
8	Lee	£13.00	42	
9	Beardsley	£14.00	35	
10	Ginola	£16.00	15	
11	Shearer	£18.00	35	
12	Ferdinand	£16.00	32	
13				

We need to find each person's pay – as the hourly rate * hours worked. You could simply type each one in, for example '=8.60*30' for Srnicek. This is time consuming and not much better than using pen and paper.
We can instead tell Excel to 'take the value in cell B2 and multiply by the value in cell C2'

	A	B	C	D	E
1	Name	Hourly Rate	Hours Worked	Pay	
2	Srnicek	£8.60	30	=b2	
3	Watson	£8.60	20		
4	Peacock	£9.00	20		
5	Albert	£11.50	25		
6	Beresford	£10.50	30		
7	Batty	£12.00	40		
8	Lee	£13.00	42		
9	Beardsley	£14.00	35		
10	Ginola	£16.00	15		
11	Shearer	£18.00	35		
12	Ferdinand	£16.00	32		
13					

Each cell is referred to by its column and row reference. To perform the calculation, start with the '=' sign to show that you want to perform a calculation. Then type the cell reference of the cell you wish to use. A box will appear around the cell.

	A	B	C	D	E
1	Name	Hourly Rate	Hours Worked	Pay	
2	Srnicek	£8.60	30	=b2*c2	
3	Watson	£8.60	20		
4	Peacock	£9.00	20		
5	Albert	£11.50	25		
6	Beresford	£10.50	30		
7	Batty	£12.00	40		
8	Lee	£13.00	42		
9	Beardsley	£14.00	35		
10	Ginola	£16.00	15		
11	Shearer	£18.00	35		
12	Ferdinand	£16.00	32		
13					

Finish off the calculation as required – the cell references are just saying "use whatever number is in this cell".

Note that although the column letters are always displayed in capitals, if you enter them in lower case it does not matter.

	D2	▼	f_x	=B2*C2	

	A	B	C	D
1	Name	Hourly Rate	Hours Worked	Pay
2	Srnicek	£8.60	30	£258.00
3	Watson	£8.60	20	
4	Peacock	£9.00	20	
5	Albert	£11.50	25	
6	Beresford	£10.50	30	
7	Batty	£12.00	40	
8	Lee	£13.00	42	
9	Beardsley	£14.00	35	
10	Ginola	£16.00	15	
11	Shearer	£18.00	35	
12	Ferdinand	£16.00	32	
13				

The result of the calculation is shown – note that the actual calculation being performed is shown in the formula bar above.

Any calculation can be performed using existing information in cells – this allows complex analysis to be undertaken relatively easily.

One huge benefit of this is that if the numbers in the data cells change, then the calculation will be updated to reflect this.

	D2	▼	f_x	=B2*C2	

	A	B	C	D
1	Name	Hourly Rate	Hours Worked	Pay
2	Srnicek	£8.60	25	£215.00
3	Watson	£8.60	20	
4	Peacock	£9.00	20	
5	Albert	£11.50	25	
6	Beresford	£10.50	30	
7	Batty	£12.00	40	
8	Lee	£13.00	42	
9	Beardsley	£14.00	35	
10	Ginola	£16.00	15	
11	Shearer	£18.00	35	
12	Ferdinand	£16.00	32	

Changing the hours worked to 25 has given an updated value in the pay column.

You can use any cell within your formulas, in the same way.

	A	B	C	D	E	F
1	Name	Hourly Rate	Hours Worked	Pay	10% Bonus	
2	Srnicek	£8.60	25	£215.00	=D2*10%	
3	Watson	£8.60	20			
4	Peacock	£9.00	20			
5	Albert	£11.50	25			

Will give

	A	B	C	D	E	F
1	Name	Hourly Rate	Hours Worked	Pay	10% Bonus	
2	Srnicek	£8.60	25	£215.00	£21.50	
3	Watson	£8.60	20			
4	Peacock	£9.00	20			
5	Albert	£11.50	25			

IMPORTANT NOTE – when entering cell references into a formula, rather than typing the reference **'B2'**, you can **LEFT-CLICK** on the cell you wish to use. This way you are less likely to type the wrong cell reference.

3.3   Copying formulas

In the previous example, a formula has been entered into cells D2 and E2. We need to perform the same calculation for the other 10 staff. It would be incredibly time consuming to have to manually enter the calculation into each cell – sometimes spreadsheets can have several thousand rows!

Fortunately Excel deals with this problem very easily. Using the same copy and paste feature seen in chapter 2, we can duplicate formulas used to speed up calculations.

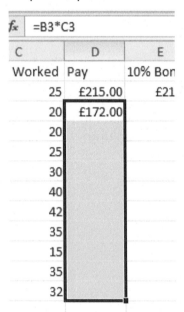

Select all the cells the formula is required in, before pasting (Ctrl-V can be used to paste the formula).

Using Autofill

Another quick way to copy formulas is to use the Autofill function explained in chapter 2. Formulas can be "dragged" up, down, left or right to copy them:

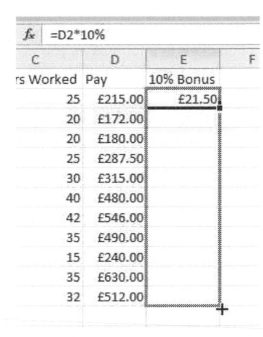

Hover the mouse over the bottom-right corner of the cell until the cursor changes to a +. Then drag the mouse in the direction you want the formulas copied, and let go of the mouse button.

Shortcut

Instead of dragging the Autofill box down, **DOUBLE CLICK** to automatically copy formulas down to the bottom of a block of cells.

3.4 Operators and the order of precedence

You are going to use simple mathematical functions to analyse your data but in order that you can do this you need to understand the order of priority given to each function. Excel follows the same mathematical rules. Below is a list of the order of precedence (priority). This is not the full list and later on during the course the full order of precedence will be shown.

Operator	Symbol	Order of Precedence
Brackets	()	1
Multiplication	*	2
Division	/	2
Addition	+	3
Subtraction	-	3

The order of precedence determines which operators Excel will use first in its calculations. It can be seen above that Excel will calculate a formula that contains multiplication or division before it calculates and addition or subtraction. By inserting brackets around part of a formula it forces Excel to calculate the content of the brackets first, followed by the remainder of the formula. You can have multiple sets of brackets in a formula as you will see in later chapters when you deal with more complex calculations.

Important

You may have come across the phrase BODMAS during a maths class. This stands for Brackets Off, Divide, Multiply, Add, Subtract – the order of precedence.

Continuing with the same example, we can demonstrate the order of precedence. We need to calculate the tax each person will pay, as 20% of their total pay.

To calculate this using one formula we need to add up two cells, and then multiply the total by 20%. However, due to the order of operations, care must be taken.

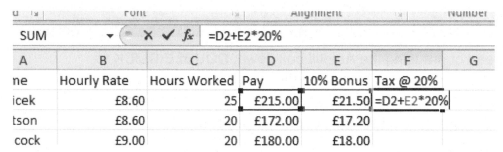

It would be tempting to type the above, as this is what we're trying to do – add up the two cells then multiply by 20%. However, Excel reads this as:

Multiply E2 by 20%, and then add on D2.

So the answer comes out as £219.30

To get round this problem, you must use brackets – put the calculation you want to happen first in brackets, to force the order as required. So:

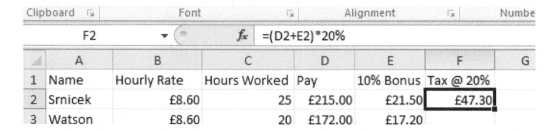

It's often worth sense checking the result of a calculation – a simple typo can give unpredictable results!

3.5 Calculation of percentage

To calculate percentages you can use:

Simple mathematical formula (note formula bar) or format the cells as percentages. The percentage format can be found on the numbers tab of 'Format Cells'.

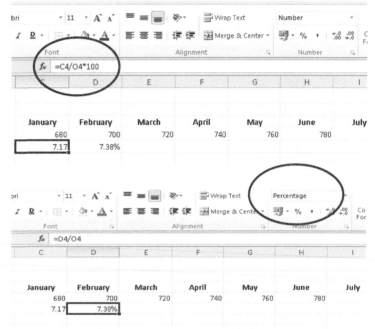

Alternatively it can be found on the format toolbar as a **%** icon.

3.6 Sorting data

Sometimes you will need to change the order of your data so that it is sorted according to your requirements. This can be performed quickly and easily, using the Sort function, located in both the **Home** tab and the **Data** tab.

To sort, select the data you wish to sort, and click on the **Sort** button.

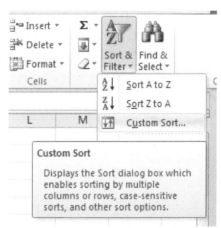

Sort A to Z and Z to A will sort data into either ascending order or descending order. This may not be what you need, so Custom Sort is usually what is required.

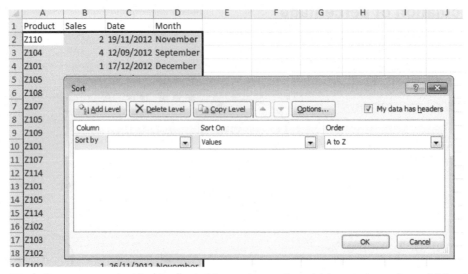

The Sort menu is displayed. Your data should have headers (titles), but if it doesn't, uncheck the check box.

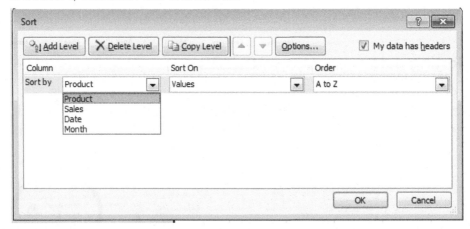

Select the column you wish to sort by, and click OK. The data will be sorted.

You may wish to sort by one column, and then another. For example, with this data set, we might want to have the transactions grouped by product, then by sales volume. This is also done with a custom sort:

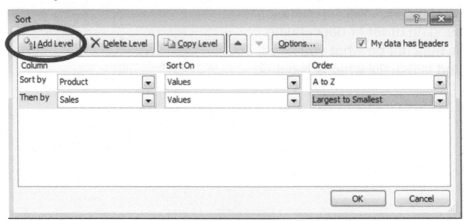

4 Page presentation and printing

4.1 Headers and footers

Headers and Footers are used to provide information in a document such as document titles, data owner, version numbers, page numbers, dates etc. **These are essential** as you may be asked to add headers or footers to your work for your SDST assessment.

To add them, use the **Insert** tab, then **Header & Footer**.

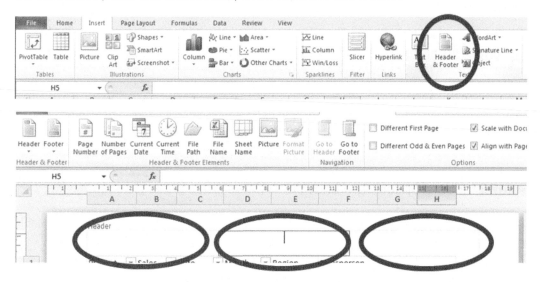

You will be taken to the Header – the page is split into three sections, where you can type in the header required. You can also select from the **Header & Footer Elements** in the Ribbon. These are fairly self-explanatory, but nothing too complicated is required for your assessment.

To edit the **Footer**, either navigate to the bottom of the page and click in the footer, or click the **Go to Footer** button.

4.2 Page Margins, Page Breaks and Orientation

All three of these options can be adjusted from the **Page Layout** tab.

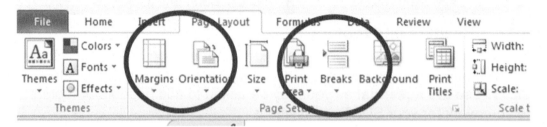

Margins

To prepare documents so that they are visually pleasing – especially for printing – you need to set the page margins. Select the **Margins** button.

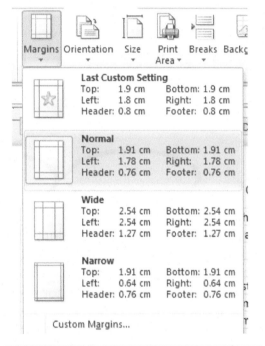

A few standard options are shown.

For more flexibility select the **Custom Margins** option.

Each individual margin can be adjusted as required.

Once you have selected your margins these will be indicated on your worksheet by broken dashed lines.

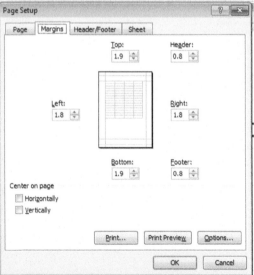

Page Breaks

With your margins set, Excel will automatically insert a break in the data so that the right amount of data is displayed on a page. However, you will find that sometimes a natural break in the data is apparent and that you want to insert your own 'Page Break'. Select the **Breaks** button.

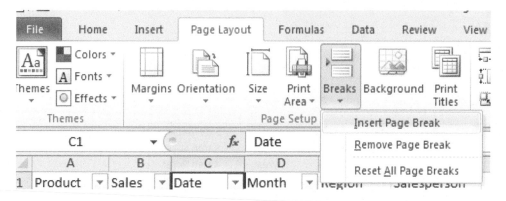

Use this to add or remove breaks as required – select the area on the sheet you would like the new page to start, and **Insert Page Break**. You can also view (and edit) page breaks in **Page Break Preview** mode. In the **View** tab, select **Page Break Preview**.

To return to normal view at any stage, select the **Normal** button just to the left of Page Break Preview.

Orientation

There are 2 ways to orientate your worksheet: Portrait or Landscape.

Excel defaults to 'Portrait', but sometimes it is better to view your document in 'Landscape'. Viewing in this way allows you to view more columns [but fewer rows] on a page.

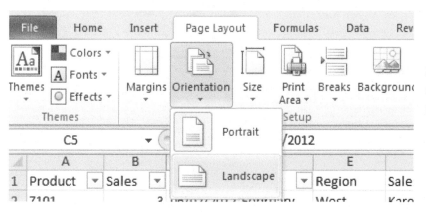

Select the orientation required.

4.3 Set Print Area

Sometimes you may want to print only part of a document. This is quite easy to do. Simply highlight the cells you wish to print, and click the **Set Print Area** button on the **Page Layout** tab.

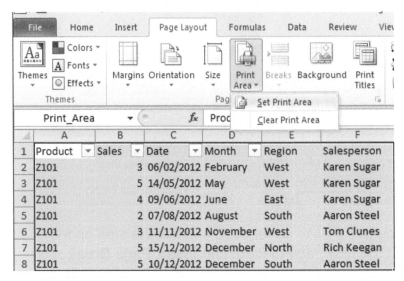

Choose **Clear Print Area** to remove this setting.

4.4 Fitting the data onto one or more sheets

One of the most useful features regarding printing is the ability to specify how many pages you want your data to appear on. Excel will then change the size of the font accordingly. Obviously this has practical limits – if you try and squeeze 1,000 lines of data onto one page, it will be impossible to read! However, it is invaluable for making your work look professional and user-friendly.

One way to do this is using the **Page Setup** menu. This is accessed by clicking on the arrow in the bottom corner of the Page Setup section of the **Page Layout** menu.

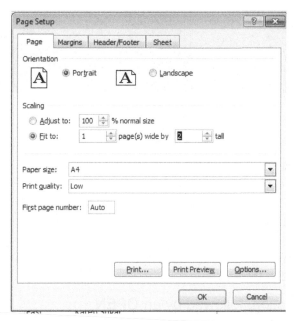

Several of the options already discussed can also be edited in this useful menu.

Use the **Fit to** option to select the number of pages required.

Use Print Preview to check that the final printout will look as desired.

4.5 Print preview and printing

Print preview has changed since Excel 2007. Rather than being a separate window view, Print Preview is found within the **File** tab, by clicking **Print**.

Having made all the adjustments to the data, format etc you will be in a position to print your document. Before you do this you should review it one more time – just to make sure. This is 'Print Preview'. When you are happy that your document is in the condition that you want it to be then you are in a position to 'Print'.

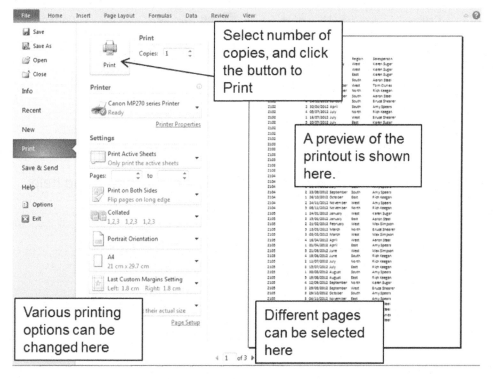

5 Excel functions

5.1 Functions

Functions are specific words which tell Excel to perform much more than just adding up a couple of cell values. They range from the relatively simple functions like **SUM**, which we shall see in a moment, to more complicated tools.

Using a function

As mentioned at the start of the previous chapter, to enter a function into a cell, always start with an **EQUALS SIGN** first.

You then type the **NAME** of the function, followed by an **OPEN BRACKET** '('.

The **ARGUMENTS** of the function are then required. These tell Excel exactly what to do, and depend on the function required. If more than one argument is needed, they must be separated by a **COMMA**.

The function is ended with a **CLOSE BRACKET** ')'.

5.2 The Insert Function button

A great way of getting used to functions within Excel is the **Insert Function** button *ƒx* located just above the column names.

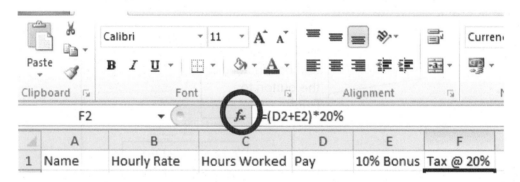

Clicking this button brings up the **Insert Function** menu, which can help work out which function is required.

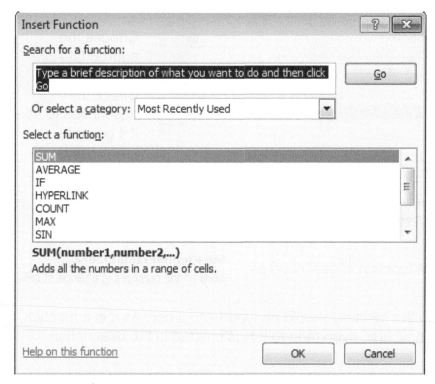

This allows you to type in – in plain English, what you require, and several options will be provided based on your search.

Using **Insert Function** also provides a more user-friendly way of entering the calculation you require, as we shall see.

5.3 SUM

SUM is probably the most commonly used function in Excel. As the name suggests, it is used to add up a selection of numbers. As discussed previously, you could use the **Insert Function** button:

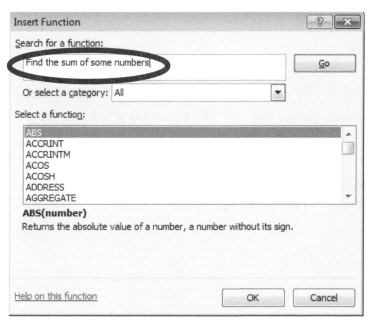

Type in what you require and click the **Go** button.

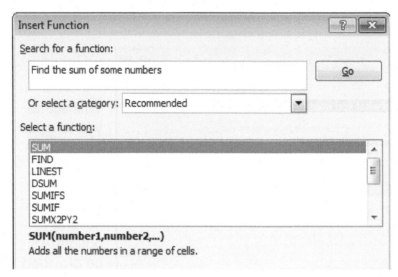

Choose the appropriate formula. Check the description to see if it going to perform the correct function.

To use the **SUM** function is described as:

SUM(number1,number2,...)
Adds all the numbers in a range of cells.

This shows how the function should be typed into a cell. As it is a function, you start with an '=' first, even though this is omitted in the description.

Number1,number2,... are the **ARGUMENTS**. In the case of SUM, these are the numbers (or cells) you wish to add. Each number you wish to add should be separated by a **comma**. For example, typing

=SUM(3,5)

will return the value 8. You can do this for any number of additions, and it is no different to using **+**, as in chapter 4.

Just like using **+**, you can also subtract cell values. In the example below, we want to find Net Pay as the sum of Pay and Bonus, less Tax; this can be done using SUM:

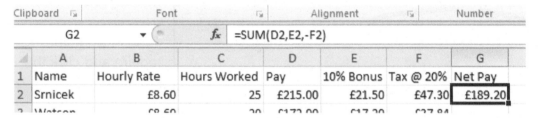

Note the minus sign before the F2 reference to indicate a subtraction. We could have done this without SUM, by typing

=D2+E2-F2

SUM is really useful when you have many numbers to add up – take the following example:

	A	B	C	D	E	F	G
1	Name	Hourly Rate	Hours Worked	Pay	10% Bonus	Tax @ 20%	Net Pay
2	Srnicek	£8.60	25	£215.00	£21.50	£47.30	£189.20
3	Watson	£8.60	20	£172.00	£17.20	£37.84	£151.36
4	Peacock	£9.00	20	£180.00	£18.00	£39.60	£158.40
5	Albert	£11.50	25	£287.50	£28.75	£63.25	£253.00
6	Beresford	£10.50	30	£315.00	£31.50	£69.30	£277.20
7	Batty	£12.00	40	£480.00	£48.00	£105.60	£422.40
8	Lee	£13.00	42	£546.00	£54.60	£120.12	£480.48
9	Beardsley	£14.00	35	£490.00	£49.00	£107.80	£431.20
10	Ginola	£16.00	15	£240.00	£24.00	£52.80	£211.20
11	Shearer	£18.00	35	£630.00	£63.00	£138.60	£554.40
12	Ferdinand	£16.00	32	£512.00	£51.20	£112.64	£450.56
13	Total						
14							

We now wish to put Total figures into columns C, D, E, F and G. Using the methods already discussed, we would either type:

=C2+C3+C4....+C12

Or

=SUM(C2,C3,C4,...,C12)

Neither of which is ideal – nor would it be practical if we had a list of hundreds of numbers to add up. Fortunately, Excel has an easy solution – rather than referring to an individual cell, we can refer to a **RANGE** of cells. We want to add the block of cells from C2 to C12, and would write that as **C2:C12** (the **:** indicating a range). Our **SUM** would be:

=SUM(C2:C12)

However, it is worth looking at how to enter this into a cell.

Direct cell entry

If you know the function required (as we do here), you can just type it in to the cell directly, as follows:

0	Ginola	£10.00	15	£240.00	£24.00	£52.80	£211.2
1	Shearer	£18.00	35	£630.00	£63.00	£138.60	£554.4
2	Ferdinand	£16.00	32	£512.00	£51.20	£112.64	£450.5
3	Total		=sum				

fx SUM   Adds all the numbers in a range of cells
fx SUMIF
fx SUMIFS
fx SUMPRODUCT

As you type, Excel will suggest possible functions. Note again the equals sign to start the function.

2	Ferdinand	£16.00	32	£512.00	£5
3	Total		=sum(		

SUM(**number1**, [number2], ...)

Open a bracket to enter the arguments. Note that the required format for the function is shown – **number1** is highlighted in bold showing that Excel is expecting you to enter the first number here. This becomes especially useful with more complex functions, as it helps you work out which part of the function you are on.

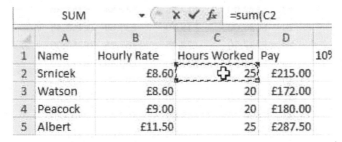

Left-click (and hold) on the first cell you wish to include. Note the formula is updated.

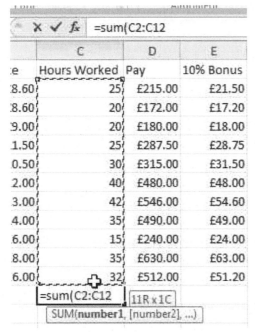

Drag the mouse down to the last cell you wish to include – the formula is automatically updated with the correct syntax. This saves you having to remember how to type the cell reference.

The box around the cells gives a visual display of the cells selected.

Release the mouse button to continue.

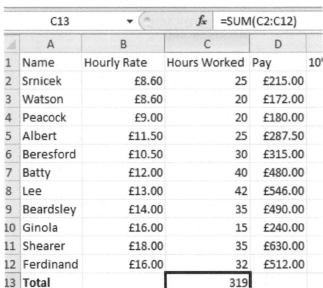

Close the bracket and press **Enter** to finish the formula. The correct answer will be shown.

Using Insert Function

Although **SUM** is relatively straightforward to use, it's worth seeing how using **Insert Function** gives a different way of entering formulae.

To enter the sum into cell D13, after selecting the **SUM** function from the **Insert Function** menu:

Number1 has already been populated with the required range – D2:D12. Clicking **OK** would give the required answer. You could also simply type in the numbers or range required into the Number1 box.

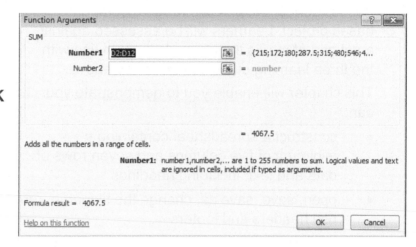

5.4 Autosum

Autosum is a useful shortcut to perform any of the above functions (and a few others) quickly and easily. The **Autosum** button can be found in the top right of the **Home** menu.

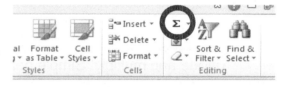

Instead of entering the function in the normal way, click in the destination cell and click the autosum button.

Excel will put in a SUM function, and guess at the cells required.

If these are incorrect, you can reselect the cells needed in the normal way.

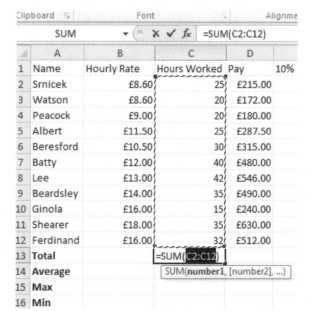

	A	B	C	D	
1	Name	Hourly Rate	Hours Worked	Pay	10%
2	Srnicek	£8.60	25	£215.00	
3	Watson	£8.60	20	£172.00	
4	Peacock	£9.00	20	£180.00	
5	Albert	£11.50	25	£287.50	
6	Beresford	£10.50	30	£315.00	
7	Batty	£12.00	40	£480.00	
8	Lee	£13.00	42	£546.00	
9	Beardsley	£14.00	35	£490.00	
10	Ginola	£16.00	15	£240.00	
11	Shearer	£18.00	35	£630.00	
12	Ferdinand	£16.00	32	£512.00	
13	Total		=SUM(C2:C12)		
14	Average		SUM(number1, [number2], ...)		
15	Max				
16	Min				

6 Level 1 assessment requirements

6.1 AAT assessment guidance

Assessment of the unit is through a computer based project. Learners will be assessed against a set grid of marks that rewards them in line with the three learning outcomes identified above.

This chapter will enable you to demonstrate you can:

- construct a spreadsheet containing a minimum of five columns and seven rows of data and text, including headings

- open, save, save as, change the filename, rename a worksheet and use headers and footers

- copy and paste data across different worksheets within the same workbook.

- add, edit, insert and/or delete data, columns and rows

- use the functions confidently to create the required output. These functions and formulas include sum, total, autosum, add, subtract, divide and multiply. Simple percentages may be tested by asking the learner to multiply an increase or decrease in percentage for example 10%, 0.10 or 110%.

- alter the following: font type, font colour, font size, bold, italics, underline, double underline, borders, shading, wrap text, currency, 1000 separator, decimal places, align text and figures

- use the following assumed skills: spell check, add delete rows/columns, edit and undo functions.

- select the most appropriate page layout (for example portrait or landscape), add a header or footer, date and time stamp and be able to change margins, print on one page or scale to fit on one page

- produce readable printouts as part of the assessment in order to be deemed competent.

You are further required to be able to identify, change and format charts and graphs, which will be covered in the following chapter. This includes using colour schemes or pattern fills to ensure discrete representations of data appear distinct from each other when printing in black and white, adding a title, axis titles, legends and scales to line charts or column charts, and add legends and percentages to pie charts, moving and resizing the chart and printing an isolated chart or graph.

Spreadsheet charts and graphs

Introduction

This chapter will guide you on how to create a number of different graphs and how to move and change these charts and graphs within the spreadsheet, therefore meeting the final assessment criteria referenced in the previous chapter. We will be looking at several types of charts and their construction, formatting and location.

In essence there is very little difference between a chart and a graph and the term is interchangeable.

KNOWLEDGE
2 Use appropriate formulas and tools to summarise spreadsheet information
3 Select and use appropriate tools and techniques to present spreadsheet information effectively

CONTENTS
1   Creating charts and graphs

1 Creating charts and graphs

1.1 Excel charts and graphs

Within Excel there are two basic ways to display charts and graphs. There is no right or wrong way, it is down to user preference. It is also a simple matter to switch between the two types.

1 **Chart Sheet** – here the chart or graph becomes the entire worksheet.

2 **Embedded** – here the chart or graph is located on the sheet that contains the data. The chart can be moved around to suit the user.

The easiest way to create a chart in Excel is to **Select** the **Data** you wish to chart, then go to the **Insert** tab, and select the **Chart** you wish to insert.

You can also highlight the data you want in your chart and **press F11**. Excel will create a default (column) chart on a chart sheet.

1.2 Types of charts and graphs

You need to be aware of the following types of graph:

- Bar and Column charts.
- Pie and Doughnut charts.
- Single and double line graphs.

Bar and Column charts

Bar and column charts are used to display and compare the number, frequency or other measure for different discrete categories of data. They are one of the most commonly used types of graph because they are simple to create and very easy to interpret. They are also a flexible chart type and there are several variations of the standard bar chart including component bar charts, and compound bar charts.

Bar charts are useful for displaying data that are classified into categories.

Bar charts are also useful for displaying data that include categories with negative values, because it is possible to position the bars below and above the x-axis.

The chart is constructed such that the lengths of the different bars are proportional to the size of the category they represent. The x-axis represents the different categories and so has no scale. In order to emphasise the fact that the categories are discrete, a gap is left between the bars on the x-axis. The y-axis does have a scale and this indicates the units of measurement.

Single and double line graphs

Line charts are used to plot continuous data and are very useful for showing trends. The more **data series** there are the more lines you can have on your graph.

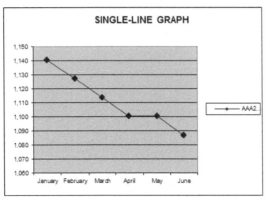
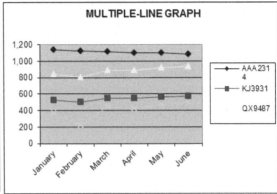

Multiple graph types on one chart

Also known as **Combination Charts** these charts must consist of at least two data series. With this chart type you can have either two graph types on **one** axis or insert a second **value** or 'Y' axis.

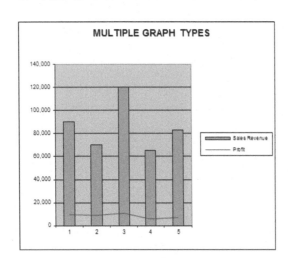
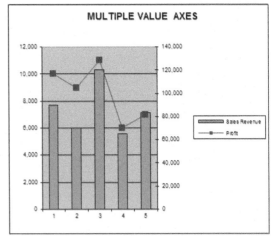

1.3 Creating a chart or graph

Select the data you wish to graph, and on the **Insert** tab, select the chart type you want.

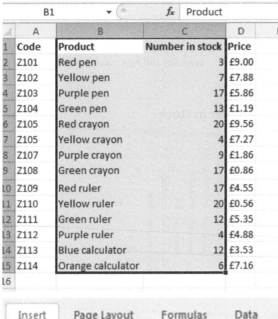

Select the data, then find the chart type you are after.

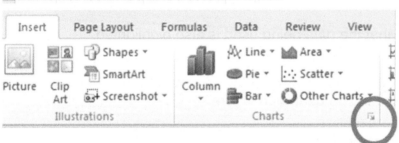

If you cannot see the chart you need, click the little arrow in the corner of the **Charts** menu, and all available charts will be shown.

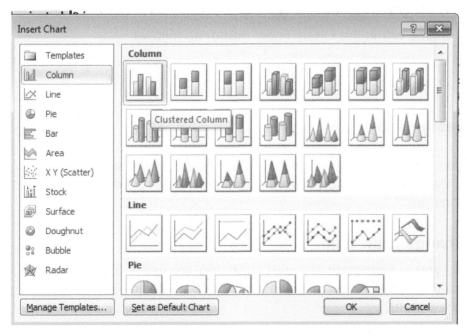

So, if you are asked for a **Clustered Column chart**, and do not know what it is – go into this menu and hover over the options to find what you need. Click **OK** once you have found what you need, and the chart will be shown.

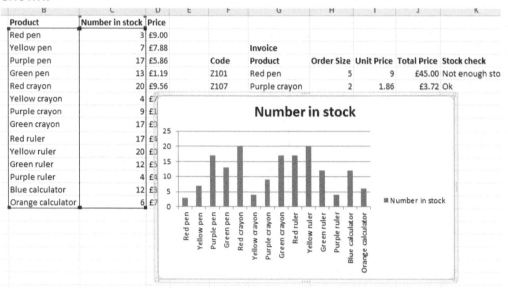

You can also see that the data being used is also highlighted.

As shown, creating a chart is not difficult – what may prove more difficult is getting it to look exactly how you want it to. There are many options available, and these will be dealt with in turn.

1.4 The chart tools tabs

When you create a chart, or have one selected, the chart tools tabs will become available on the Ribbon. These will allow you to change the features of your chart.

There are 3 tabs within the Chart Tools menu, as follows:

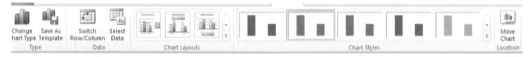

1.5 Design Tab

This is to do with the fundamental features of your chart – what sort of chart it is, the data used and where it is shown on your spreadsheet. The main options are:

1.6 Change chart type

This allows you to change the type of chart you are using. The menu showing all available charts is shown, and can be selected in the same way as a new chart.

1.7 Select data

This is a very important menu. It allows you to change the data being used, or add new **Series** (data sets) to the chart.

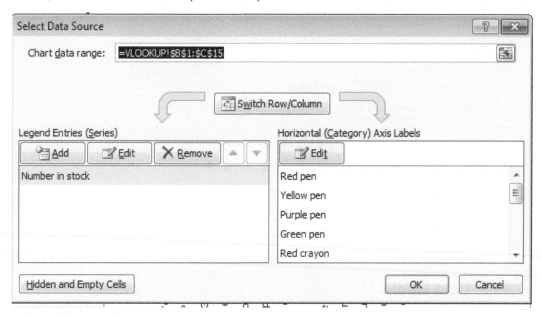

The data range, as shown here, is the original data that was selected to draw the graph. This can be edited if more data is added, or if you wish to add another set of data to the graph.

1.8 Move chart

This allows you to switch between an **embedded** chart and a **Chart Sheet**. Simply click on the **Move Chart** button to change the location of your chart.

1.9 Layout Tab

From the point of view of the SDST assessment, this is probably the most important menu. This is where you can change many of the key visual features of your chart, such as titles and legends.

1.10 Chart title, axis title and Legend

As the name suggests, this allows you to add or remove a main title for your chart (there are also options as to where and how the title is displayed), allows you to add or remove titles for both axes and add, remove or change the location of the Legend. The **Legend** is the 'key' which explains what the different colours or bars on the graph correspond to.

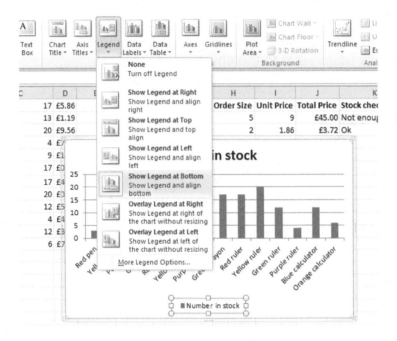

1.11 Data labels

These show the actual values of the data points on the graph. You can turn them on or off, as well as where they appear on the chart.

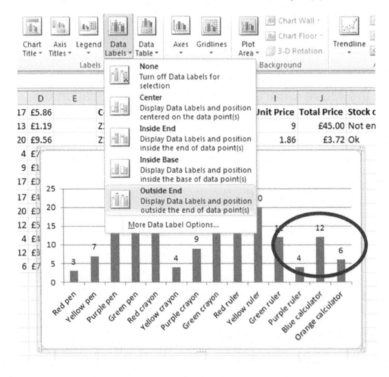

1.12   Data table

A data table shows the actual data points being used to make the chart – like data labels but shown beneath the chart. Use this option to add/remove a data table, with or without a legend (key). The example below shows a data table with a legend key.

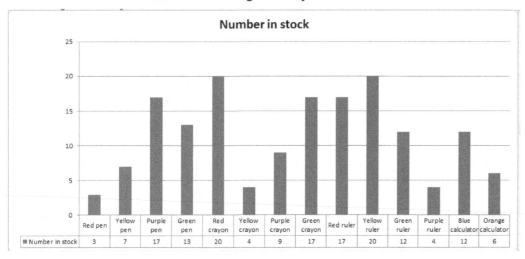

1.13   Format Tab

This tab allows you to change the format of any aspect of your graph – colours, thickness of lines and several other formatting options. Select (left-click on) the area of the graph you need to format and then select the option you need.

1.14   Adding another data set

More data series can be added if you want to show more information on your graph. This is done within the **Select Data** option. Click **Add** to add more data.

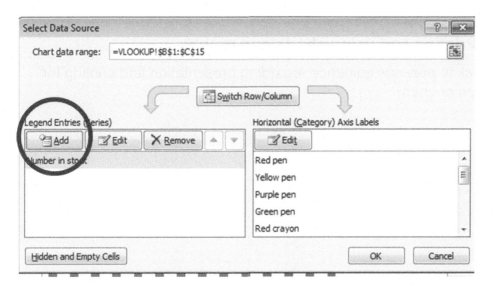

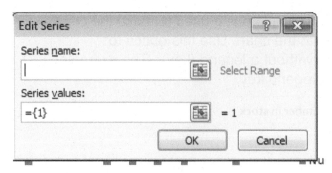

The **Series name** box allows you to select the name for your new data set – this can either be a cell reference or typed value.

The **Series values** represent the actual data points, which can also be selected.

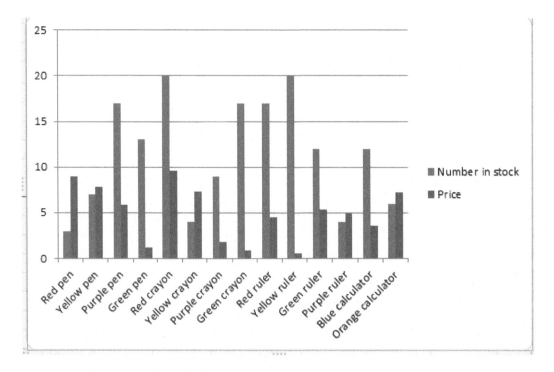

The new data series is shown on the graph.

1.15 Printing and using charts and graphs

Refer back to previous guidance regarding presentation and printing for your graph or chart.

Mock Assessment 1 – Bookkeeping and Accounts

Introduction

The following is a Mock Assessment to be attempted in exam conditions.

You should attempt and aim to complete EVERY task.

Read every task carefully to make sure you understand what is required.

Where the date is relevant, it is given in the task.

Both minus signs and brackets can be used to indicate negative numbers UNLESS task instructions say otherwise.

You must use a full stop to indicate a decimal point.

Time allowed: 2 hours

1 Mock Assessment Questions

Task 1

There are main differences between the roles of bookkeepers and accountants within an organisation.

a) Which of the following statements regarding the differences in these roles are True and which are False? Tick the correct answer.

Statement	True	False
A bookkeeper will be dealing with day to day transactions		
An accountant will be concentrating on the overall financial information		
A bookkeeper, with study and hard work can achieve the role of the accountant		
The bookkeeper position is a job with no career prospects		

b) Show whether the tasks below would be carried out by an accountant or by a bookkeeper in a large organisation.

Link the task with the appropriate job role by drawing a line between the two.

Task   **Job role**

| Authorising a loan to buy a new piece of machinery |

| Performing the bank reconciliation | | Bookkeeper |

| Reviewing the cash position of the organisation |

| Printing off a sales credit note | | Accountant |

c) Which of the following is a numerical code? Tick the correct box(es).

Code	Numerical code?
SMITH	
12LG5	
HAGE	
15796	
ALL01	

d) Below is statement about batch control. Is it True or False?

Statement	True	False
Batch control does not save time as items, like sales invoices, are recorded as and when received.		

Task 2

Goods were received by ZDT Ltd on 13 May in accordance with purchase order below.

ZDT Ltd was given a 15% trade discount and a 2% settlement discount for payment within five days.

ZDT Ltd
22 New Ash
Grandy GD1 2PX

Purchase Order No 6866

Be Goods Ltd
179 Alter Way
Darchester
DD17 9LL   13 May 20X5

Please supply 10 boxes of product P21 at £15.00 per box.

---

a) Complete the invoice to be sent to ZDT Ltd by:

- Entering the correct details in the first three columns
- Entering the correct invoice amounts to the final three columns
- Entering the amount of trade discount at the bottom of the invoice

Be Goods Ltd
179 Alter Way
Darchester DD17 9LL

To: ZDT Ltd
178 New Ash
Grandy
GD1 2PX

13 May 20X5
Purchase Order No 6866

SALES INVOICE 256

Quantity of units	Product code	Price per unit £	Total amount after discount	VAT £	Total £

Terms of payment 2% discount for payment within seven days:

This invoice includes a trade discount of: %.

It is important that sales invoices are carefully checked for accuracy before being sent to customers.

b)   Check the sales invoice and identify TWO errors from the list below.

Error	✔
Customer name and address	
Date of invoice	
Purchase order number	
Terms of payment	

ZDT Ltd sent a purchase order to the supplier and after the goods were delivered the supplier sent ZDT Ltd an invoice.

c)   What will be the next action on the part of **ZDT Ltd**?

Action	✔
Send a credit note	
Send Statement of account	
Send a cheque	
Send a bank statement	

Task 3

Three sales credit notes have been partially entered into the sales returns day book.

GGD Ltd
117 Vinefield Place
Warminster
Kent WA1 1BB

Credit Note 552	**Date:1 June 20XX**
	£
250 products GUP @ £2.00	500.00
VAT @ 20%	100.00
Gross amount refunded	600.00

Terms: Net monthly account

Day Associates
2 London Road
Becksley
Kent BE7 9MN

Credit Note 35	**Date:10 June 20XX**
	£
24 products Y12 @ £5.75	138.00
VAT @ 20%	27.60
Gross amount refunded	165.60

Terms: Net monthly account

Cohen PLC
25 Main Road
Rexsome
Herefordshire HR2 6PS

Credit Note 1168	**Date:23 June 20XX**
	£
80 products Y12 @ £7.10	568.00
VAT @ 20%	113.60
Gross amount refunded	681.60

Terms: Net monthly account

Complete the entries in the sales returns day book by inserting the credit note number and the gross, VAT and net amounts for each credit note.

Sales returns day book

Date 20XX	Details	Credit note number	Total £	VAT £	Net £
1 June	GGD Ltd				
10 June	Day Associates				
23 June	Cohen PLC				

Task 4

These are the totals from a sales day book for one month

Date 20XX	Details	Invoice number	Total £	VAT £	Net £
	Totals		2,118.72	353.12	1,765.60

a) What will be the entries in the general ledger? Enter the account name from the list below, enter the amount and tick either debit or credit.

General ledger

Account name	Amount	Debit ✓	Credit ✓

Pick list

Sales	Sales returns	Sales ledger control account
Purchases	Purchase returns	VAT

One of the sales invoices in the sales day book was from L Helps for £72.00 plus VAT of £14.40.

b) What will be the entries in the sales ledger?

Account name	Amount	Debit ✓	Credit ✓

Task 5

The petty cash book below is a book of prime entry, and part of the double entry bookkeeping system.

The imprest amount is £150 and is restored at the beginning of every month. There are two petty cash vouchers to be entered into the petty cash book.

PETTY CASH VOUCHER	
29 June 20XX	**No 521**
	£
Window cleaner	20.00
VAT not applicable	————
Gross amount refunded	20.00

PETTY CASH VOUCHER	
30 June 20XX	**No 522**
	£
Fuel for delivery van	19.20
VAT	3.84
Gross amount refunded	23.04

a) Enter the above transactions into the partially completed petty cash book below.

b) Total the petty cash book and show the balance carried down.

Petty cash book

Details	Amount £	Details	Amount £	VAT £	Motor expenses £	Sundry expenses £
Balance b/d	150.00	Motor fuel	24.00	4.00	20.00	
		Motor oil	23.88	3.98	19.90	
		Window cleaner				
		Motor fuel				
		Balance c/d				

It is important to cross check the totals in the petty cash book to ensure accuracy.

c)   Complete the following sentence by removing (putting a line through) one of the highlighted word(s):

When the total expenditure column is subtracted from the balance b/d figure the resulting amount **should/should not** be equal to the amount of money in the petty cash box.

The total of the analysis columns in the petty cash book will be transferred to the general ledger.

d)   Will the petty cash expenses be recorded on the debit or credit side of the accounts in the general ledger?

	✓
Debit	
Credit	

At the start of the next month cash was withdrawn from the bank to restore the imprest amount.

e)   What was the amount of cash withdrawn from the bank to restore the imprest amount?

Answer: £ [   ]

Task 6

When an organisation receives a bank statement, it is used to update the cashbook.

Referring to the bank statement and the cashbook below:

a)   Check the items on the bank statement against the items in the cashbook

b)   Enter the ONE lodgement from a credit customer that is in the bank statement but not in the cashbook

c)   Enter the ONE cash purchase of £150 plus VAT of £30 that is in the bank statement but not in the cashbook.

d)   Total and balance the cashbook

Bank statement

Date 20XX	Details	Paid out £	Paid in £	Balance £
01 Jun	Balance b/d			5,168
03 Jun	Counter credit – R Brown		250	5,418
9 June	Counter credit – A Bate		425	5,843
13 Jun	Cheque – Trafalgar plc	120		5,723
14 Jun	Cheque – P Tuller	138		5,585
19 Jun	Counter credit – R Brown		300	5,885
20 Jun	Cheque – Printer Palace	400		5,485
21 Jun	Cheque - English Electrics	180		5,305
26 Jun	Counter credit – C Beamer		175	5,480
27 Jun	Counter credit – R Giggs		180	5,660

Cash book

Details	Bank	VAT	Cash sales	Sales ledger	Details	Bank	VAT	Cash purchases	Purchase ledger
Balance b/d	5,168				Trafalgar plc	120	20	100	
R Brown	250			250	P Tuller	138	23	115	
A Bate	425	70	355		Printer Palace	400			400
R Brown	300			300	English Electrics				
R Giggs	180	30	150		Balance c/d				
C Beamer									
Totals					Totals				

Task 7

These are the totals from the credit side of the cash book for one month. The cash book is a book of prime entry and part of the double entry bookkeeping system.

There was no opening bank balance at the start of the month.

Cash book – credit side

Details	Bank £	VAT £	Purchase ledger £	Cash purchases £
Totals	14,225	225	6,755	7,245

a)   What will be the THREE entries in the general ledger?

Account name	Amount £	Debit ✓	Credit ✓

One of the cash payments was to a credit supplier   BKL Ltd, for £4,876.

b)   What will be the entry in the purchase ledger?

Purchase ledger

Account name	Amount £	Debit ✓	Credit ✓

Task 8

It is important to regularly reconcile the bank statement with the cashbook. Returning to the cash book and the bank statement below:

a)   Identify the TWO outstanding lodgements that are included in the cashbook but missing from the bank statement.

b)   Identify the one unpresented cheque that is included in the cash book but missing from the bank statement.

c)   Complete the bank reconciliation statement, do NOT use minus signs or brackets to show negative amounts.

d)   Calculate the balance of the cash book and ensure it matches the balance as per cash book you have calculated in the bank reconciliation statement. Do NOT make any entries in the cash book.

Cash book

Date	Details	Bank £	Date	Cheque number	Details	Bank £
01 Aug	Balance b/d	5,776	01 Aug	027651	Franley Ltd	350
05 Aug	M Geyzers	2,150	02 Aug	027652	Moonley Ltd	667
20 Aug	Adison plc	765	03 Aug	027653	English Electrics	1,475
21 Aug	Diamond plc	190	16 Aug	027654	Shore Interiors	3,380
25 Aug	Avril Trading	810	18 Aug	027655	Waterson plc	665
26 Aug	Railing Associates	667	22 Aug	027656	Planters Products	450
26 Aug	Barry Cord	448				

Bank statement

Date	Details	Paid out £	Paid in £	Balance
01 Aug	Balance b/d			5,776
05 Aug	Cheque 027651	350		5,426
08 Aug	Cheque 027653	1,475		3,951
10 Aug	Counter credit – M Geyzers		2,150	6,101
10 Aug	Cheque 027652	667		5,434
20 Aug	Cheque 027654	3,380		2,054
25 Aug	Counter credit – Diamond plc		190	2,244
28 Aug	Counter credit – Avril Trading		810	3,054
29 Aug	Cheque 027656	450		2,604
31 Aug	Counter credit – Barry Cord		448	3,052

Bank reconciliation statement

Balance as per bank statement	£
Add:	
	£
	£
Total to add	£
Less:	
	£
Total to subtract	£
Balance as per cash book	£

Task 9

The following account is in the purchase ledger at the close of day on 31 August:

Billy Buster

Date 20XX	Details	Amount £	Date 20XX	Details	Amount £
03 Aug	Credit note 57	383	01 Aug	Balance b/d	2,556
04 Aug	Bank	209	25 Aug	Purchase invoice 1558	393
27 Aug	Credit note 59	530	28 Aug	Purchase invoice 1582	779
			29 Aug	Purchase invoice 1601	980

a) What will be the balance brought down on 01 September?

Amount £	Debit ✓	Credit ✓

The following account is in the general ledger at the close of day on 31 August.

b) Insert the balance carried down at 31 August together with date and details.

c) Insert the totals.

d) Insert the balance brought down at 1 September together with date and details.

Cash

Date 20XX	Details	Amount £	Date 20XX	Details	Amount £
01 Aug	**Balance b/d**	1,050	02 Aug	Bank	750
17 Aug	Sales	543	24 Aug	Bank	382

Task 10

Below is a list of balances to be transferred to the trial balance.

Place the figures in the debit or credit columns, as appropriate, and total each column.

Account name	Amount £	Debit £	Credit £
Capital	4,922		
Cash at bank	5,655		
General expenses	1,765		
Petty cash	50		
Purchases	4,334		
Purchase ledger control	1,880		
Sales	7,870		
Sales ledger control	3,326		
Purchase returns	324		
VAT (owing to HM Revenue & Customs)	782		
Totals			

Task 11

Small organisations may use a single entry bookkeeping system to record accounting transactions, while larger organisations will use the double entry system.

a)   Complete the sentences below by circling the correct words

When a double entry bookkeeping system is used **one entry/two entries** will be used per transaction.

A **day book/spreadsheet** may be the record of transactions.

The advantage of keeping records in the double entry bookkeeping system is that the records are **complete/incomplete** but the disadvantage is that it can be **time consuming/quick**.

b)   Show the meaning of each of the accounting terms below by drawing a line between the left hand box and the appropriate right hand box.

Accounting Terms	Meaning
Cash sales	The purchase of goods with payment within an agreed period of time
Cash purchases	A group of contacts from who purchases are made.
Customers	A group of contacts to whom goods are sold.
Suppliers	The purchase of goods with immediate payment.
Credit sales	The sale of goods with immediate effect.
Credit purchases	The sales of goods with payment in an agreed period of time.

Task 12

a) Show the percentage amount for each of the VAT rates by drawing a line between the left hand box and the appropriate right hand box.

VAT rate	%
Zero	5%
Standard rate	0%
Reduced rate	20%

Some organisations have to be VAT registered

b) Choose the correct option below to state when organisations have to register for VAT.

	✓
When the taxable turnover of the business reaches a certain amount	
When the organisation produces their 100th invoice.	

c) What type of business would each of the organisations below be most likely to trade as?

Tick the correct box to give the best description for each.

Organisation	Sole Trader	Partnership	Public limited company
A plumber			
Shop owned by two sisters			
A bus company			
Large business trading in many different areas			

Task 13

It is important to understand accounting terms

a)   Are the following statements true or false? Tick the appropriate box.

Statement	True	False
When a business pays the electricity bill the payment is known as expenditure.		
When a business receives revenue from sales the receipt is known as expenditure		
When a supplier receives a cheque from a customer the supplier will call it a payment		
When a customer sends a cheque to a supplier the customer will call it a payment		

It is important to understand the need for authorisation

b)   State whether the following statements regarding authorisation are True or False.

Statement	True	False
Before a cheque is issued for the purchase of goods it should be authorised by the sales manager		
Before a sales credit note is sent to a customer it should be authorised by the accountant		

Security of confidential information is the responsibility of all who work in the accounting role.

c)   Show whether the following actions should be allowed or not allowed.

Action	Allowed	NOT allowed
Give the company accountant details of amounts owed to suppliers		
Give suppliers details of other supplier's confidential information		
Give customers details of the amounts owed by other customers		
Give HM Revenue and Customers details of payments due to them		

Mock Assessment 2 – Bookkeeping and Accounts

Introduction

The following is a Mock Assessment to be attempted in exam conditions.

You should attempt and aim to complete EVERY task.

Read every task carefully to make sure you understand what is required.

Where the date is relevant, it is given in the task.

Both minus signs and brackets can be used to indicate negative numbers UNLESS task instructions say otherwise.

You must use a full stop to indicate a decimal point.

Time allowed: 2 hours

1   Mock Assessment Questions

Task 1

There are differences between the roles of bookkeepers and accountants within an organisation.

a)   Below are some duties that are performed in an organisation. They are performed either by a bookkeeper or by an accountant. Tick the box that you think is the correct answer.

Statement	Accountant	Bookkeeper
Dealing with the Board of Directors		
Dealing with sales transactions		
Handling a simple supplier query		
Signing a £1,000,000 contract		

b)   Show whether the tasks below would be carried out by an accountant in a large organisation.

Link the task with the appropriate answer:

Task

Totalling the Cash book

Meet with the bank manager to discuss a loan

Entertain potential clients

Sign off a £5,000 credit note

Accountant

Yes

No

c) Identify which type of business structure the organisations below will typically have. Tick the correct column.

Organisation	Sole trader	Partnership	Limited company	Not for profit organisation
Local Scouts club				
Ltd company not traded on stock exchange				
Bookkeeper working for self				
Plumber				
RSPCA				
Three friends set up business to make a profit				
Council-run swimming baths				

d) Below is statement about a bookkeeping position. Is it True or False?

Statement	True	False
A bookkeeping position can lead to further prospects and a varied career.		

Task 2

Goods were received by Patel Partners on 21 October in accordance with purchase order below.

Patel Partners was given a 5% trade discount and a 2% settlement discount for payment within five days.

Patel Partners
13 Wisteria Drive
Gloucester GR1 3DD

Purchase Order No 5221

Want More Ltd
22 Meantime Way
Longshot
LS17 1TP

21 October 20X5

Please supply 100 boxes of product WIGD at £7.50 per box.

a)   Complete the invoice to be sent to Patel Partners by:
   - Entering the correct details in the first three columns
   - Entering the correct invoice amounts to the final three columns
   - Entering the amount of trade discount at the bottom of the invoice

Want More Ltd
22 Meantime Way
Longshot
LS17 1TP

To: Patel Partners
13 Wisteria Drive
Gloucester GR1 3DD

24 October 20X5
Purchase Order No 5212

SALES INVOICE 256

Quantity of units	Product code	Price per unit £	Total amount after discount	VAT £	Total £

Terms of payment 5% discount for payment within seven days:

This invoice includes a trade discount of**:**   %.

It is important that sales invoices are carefully checked for accuracy before being sent to customers.

b)   Check the sales invoice and identify TWO errors from the list below.

Error	✓
Customer name and address	
Date of invoice	
Purchase order number	
Terms of payment	

Patel Partners received invoices from their suppliers, followed by a statement of account.

c)   What will be the next action on the part of **Patel Partners**?

Action	✓
Send a credit note	
Send a statement of account	
Send a payment	
Send a bank statement	

Task 3

Three purchase invoices have been partially entered into the purchase day book.

GGD Ltd
117 Vinefield Place
Warminster
Kent WA1 1BB

Invoice 3575	Date:21 October 20XX
	£
70 units of **SPLAT** @ £12.75	892.50
VAT @ 20%	178.50
Total	1,071.00
Terms: Net monthly account	

Day Associates
2 London Road
Becksley
Kent BE7 9MN

Invoice 35   **Date:22 October 20XX**

	£
2400 units of AA12 @ £0.55	1,320.00
VAT @ 20%	264.00
Total	1,584.00

Terms: Net monthly account

Cohen PLC
25 Main Road
Rexsome
Herefordshire HR2 6PS

Invoice 1164   **Date:23 October 20XX**

	£
40 units of Y12 @ £14.20	568.00
VAT @ 20%	113.60
Total	681.60

Terms: Net monthly account

Complete the entries in the purchases day book by inserting the invoice number and the gross, VAT and net amounts for each invoice .

Purchases day book

Date 20XX	Details	Invoice	Total £	VAT £	Net £
1 June	GGD Ltd				
10 June	Day Associates				
23 June	Cohen PLC				

Task 4

These are the totals from a sales returns day book for one month

Date 20XX	Details	Invoice number	Total £	VAT £	Net £
	Totals		2,118.72	353.12	1,765.60

a)   What will be the entries in the general ledger? Enter the account name from the list below, enter the amount from the sales returns day book and tick either debit or credit.

General ledger

Account name	Amount	Debit ✓	Credit ✓

Pick list

Sales	Sales returns	Sales ledger control account
Purchases	Purchase returns	VAT

One of the sales invoices in the sales returns day book was from JT Pritchards for £123.00 plus VAT of £24.60.

b)   What will be the entries in the sales ledger?

Account name	Amount	Debit ✓	Credit ✓

Task 5

The petty cash book below is a book of prime entry, and part of the double entry bookkeeping system.

The imprest amount is £125 and is restored at the beginning of every month. There are two petty cash vouchers to be entered into the petty cash book.

PETTY CASH VOUCHER	
29 March 20XX	**No 963**
	£
Donation to local charity	25.00
VAT not applicable	_____
Gross amount refunded	25.00

PETTY CASH VOUCHER	
30 March 20XX	**No 964**
	£
Taxi fares	19.20
VAT	3.84
Gross amount refunded	23.04

a)   Enter the above transactions into the partially completed petty cash book below.

b)   Total the petty cash book and show the balance carried down.

Petty cash book

Details	Amount £	Details	Amount £	VAT £	Travel £	Sundry expenses £
Balance b/d	125.00	Motor fuel	24.00	4.00	20.00	
		Motor oil	23.88	3.98	19.90	
		Balance c/d				

It is important to cross check the totals in the petty cash book to ensure accuracy.

c) Complete the following sentence by crossing out one of the highlighted word(s):

When the total expenditure column is subtracted from the balance b/d figure the resulting amount **should/should not** be equal to the amount of money in the petty cash box.

The total of the analysis columns in the petty cash book will be transferred to the general ledger.

d) Will the amount that tops up the petty cash be recorded on the debit or credit side of the **cash book** in the general ledger?

	✓
Debit	
Credit	

At the start of the next month cash was withdrawn from the bank to restore the imprest amount.

e) What was the amount of cash withdrawn from the bank to restore the imprest amount?

Answer: £ _____

Task 6

When an organisation receives a bank statement, it is used to update the cashbook.

Referring to the bank statement and the cashbook below:

a) Check the items on the bank statement against the items in the cashbook

b) Enter the ONE cash receipt of £600 + VAT that is in the bank statement but not in the cashbook

c) Enter the ONE credit purchase that is in the bank statement but not in the cashbook.

d) Total and balance the cashbook

Bank statement

Date 20XX	Details	Paid out £	Paid in £	Balance £
01 Jun	Balance b/d			4,550
03 Jun	Counter credit – S Callaghan		75	4,625
9 June	Counter credit – B Wadhurst		800	5,425
13 Jun	Cheque – Waterloo plc	120		5,305
14 Jun	Cheque – P Umpkin	951		4,354
19 Jun	Counter credit – S Top		115	4,469
20 Jun	Cheque – Simply Stationery		70	4,539
21 Jun	Cheque - Geordie Gas	180		4,359
26 Jun	Counter credit – H.I. Light		720	5,079
27 Jun	Counter credit – R Winder		99	5,178

Cash book

Details	Bank	VAT	Cash sales	Sales ledger	Details	Bank	VAT	Cash purchases	Purchase ledger
Balance b/d	4,550				P Umpkin	951			
S Callaghan	75			75	Waterloo plc	120	20	100	
B Wadhurst	800			800					
S Top	115			115	Geordie Gas				
Simply Stationery	70			70	Balance c/d				
H.I. Light									
R Winder	99			99					
Totals					Totals				

Task 7

These are the totals from the debit side of the cash book for one month. The cash book is a book of prime entry and part of the double entry bookkeeping system.

There was no opening bank balance at the start of the month.

Cash book – debit side

Details	Bank £	VAT £	Sales ledger £	Cash sales £
Totals	15,112	512	12,384	2,216

a)   What will be the THREE entries in the general ledger?

Account name	Amount £	Debit ✓	Credit ✓

One of the cash receipts was to a credit customer JLK Ltd, for £2,885

b)   What will be the entry in the sales ledger?

Sales ledger

Account name	Amount £	Debit ✓	Credit ✓

Task 8

It is important to regularly reconcile the bank statement with the cashbook. Returning to the cash book and the bank statement below:

a)   Identify the TWO outstanding lodgements that are included in the cashbook but missing from the bank statement.

b)   Identify the one unpresented cheque that is included in the cash book but missing from the bank statement.

c)   Complete the bank reconciliation statement, do NOT use minus signs or brackets to show negative amounts.

d)   Calculate the balance of the cash book and ensure it matches the balance as per cash book you have calculated in the bank reconciliation statement. Do NOT make any entries in the cash book.

Cash book

Date	Details	Bank £	Date	Cheque number	Details	Bank £
01 July	Balance b/d	5,986	01 July	3251	Fields Ltd	325
05 July	M Gershwin	2,150	02 July	3252	Mozert Ltd	225
20 July	Amber plc	765	03 July	3253	Geordie Gas	1,754
21 July	Diamond plc	190	16 July	3254	Shoe Interiors	3,330
25 July	Vias Trading	1,810	18 July	3255	Waterman plc	675
26 July	Roos Associates	667	22 July	3256	Price Products	450
26 July	M Manigigh	448				

Bank statement

Date	Details	Paid out £	Paid in £	Balance
01 July	Balance b/d			5,986
05 July	Cheque 3251	325		5,661
08 July	Cheque 3253	1,754		3,907
10 July	Counter credit – M Gershwin		2,150	6,057
10 July	Cheque 3252	225		5,832
20 July	Cheque 3254	3,330		2,502
25 July	Counter credit – Diamond plc		190	2,692
28 July	Counter credit – ViasTrading		1,810	4,502
29 July	Cheque 3256	450		4,052
31 July	Counter credit – M Manigigh		448	4,500

Bank reconciliation statement

Balance as per bank statement	£
Add:	
	£
	£
Total to add	£
Less:	
	£
Total to subtract	£
Balance as per cash book	£

Task 9

The following account is in the sales ledger at the close of day on 31 January

Marlin Products

Date 20XX	Details	Amount £	Date 20XX	Details	Amount £
01 Jan	Balance b/d	3,498	25 Jan	Cash received	3,443
04 Jan	Invoice 96	1,115	28 Jan	Credit note C11	55
27 Jan	Invoice 97	1,530	29 Jan	Cash received	1,115

a) What will be the balance brought down on 01 February?

Amount £	Debit ✓	Credit ✓

The following account is in the general ledger at the close of day on 31 January.

b) Insert the balance carried down at 31 January together with date and details.

c) Insert the totals.

d) Insert the balance brought down at 1 February together with date and details.

Cash

Date 20XX	Details	Amount £	Date 20XX	Details	Amount £
01 Jan	Balance b/d	1,444	02 Jan	Bank	213
17 Jan	Sales	875	24 Jan	Bank	594

Task 10

Below is a list of balances to be transferred to the trial balance.

Place the figures in the debit or credit columns, as appropriate, and total each column.

Account name	Amount £	Debit £	Credit £
Capital	8,000		
Cash at bank	3,432		
General expenses	960		
Petty cash	75		
Purchases	4,500		
Purchase ledger control	1,225		
Sales	8,630		
Sales ledger control	7,220		
Sales returns	456		
VAT (owing by HM Revenue & Customs)	1,212		
Totals			

Task 11

Small organisations may use a single entry bookkeeping system to record accounting transactions, while larger organisations will use the double entry system.

a) Complete the sentences below by circling the correct words

When a single entry bookkeeping system is used **one entry/two entries** will be used per transaction.

A **day book/spreadsheet** may be the record of transactions.

The disadvantage of keeping records in the single entry bookkeeping system is that the records are **complete/incomplete** but the advantage is that it can be time **consuming/quick**.

b) Show the meaning of each of the accounting terms below by drawing a line between the left hand box and the appropriate right hand box.

Accounting Terms   **Meaning**

| daybook | Tax charge on the sale of goods and services |

| cash sale | Method of processing financial documents all together. |

| output tax | Small amounts of cash held by a business |

| Batch processing | System where petty cash is topped up to a set amount at regular intervals. |

| petty cash | The sale of goods with money received straight away |

| imprest system | Book of prime entry |

Task 12

a) Show the percentage amount for each of the VAT rates by drawing a line between the left hand box and the appropriate right hand box.

VAT rate   **%**

| Zero | 5% |

| Standard rate | 0% |

| Reduced rate | 20% |

Some organisations have to be VAT registered

b) Choose the correct option below to state when organisations have to register for VAT.

	✓
An organisation can choose to be VAT registered	
An organisation can choose NOT to be VAT registered	

c) Below are some examples of different codings used within an organisation.

Tick the correct box that you think gives the best description for each.

Code	Invoice	Credit note	Sales ledger code
66524			
CN25			
SMITH01			

Task 13

It is important to understand accounting terms

a) Are the following statements true or false? Tick the appropriate box.

Statement	True	False
When a business receives a cheque in payment of a sales invoice it is known as income.		
When a business receives revenue from sales the receipt is known as expenditure		
When an organisation issues a cheque to a supplier the supplier will call it a receipt		
When a customer sends a cheque to a supplier the customer will call it a receipt		

It is important to understand the need for authorisation

b) State whether the following statements regarding authorisation are True or False.

Statement	True	False
Before a cheque is issued for the purchase of goods it should be authorised by the accounts assistant		
Before a sales credit note is sent to a customer it should be authorised by the purchase manager		

Security of confidential information is the responsibility of all who work in the accounting role.

c) Show whether the following actions should be allowed or not allowed.

Action	Allowed	NOT allowed
Give the sales team details of amounts owed to suppliers		
Give customers details of other customer's confidential information		
Give the finance director details of the amounts owed by customers		
Give a rival business details of payments due to the organisation's suppliers		

Mock Assessment – Spreadsheet software

Introduction

You have 1 hour 45 minutes plus 15 minutes of reading time to complete this assessment.

In the assessment you will be given extra time if necessary to allow for possible delays such as printer queries and uploading documents.

There are 16 tasks in this assessment and it is important that you attempt all tasks.

1 Mock Assessment Questions

Task 1

Open a blank worksheet Save this file in an appropriate location and rename it as follows: 'your initial_surname_AAT no_dd.mm.yy_CS'.

Create a footer on the worksheet(s) that you use with your name, AAT number and the date.

Task 2

Simply Pretty sells a range of ethnic knitwear.

After a review with your supervisor it has been decided that you will be able to assist the payroll team with their data entry. Your supervisor has suggested that you start by inputting hours worked by the sales team into a spreadsheet. This will be used to calculate the staff bonuses for week 24 of the payroll year.

Open a blank worksheet and in cells A1, B1 and C1 enter the following column headings respectively: Name, Sales target, Sales actual.

Task 3

a) Fill in the spreadsheet using the data displayed below and the column headings you have already entered as part of Task 2. Identify only the relevant data and then input into the appropriate rows and columns.

b) Rename the worksheet **'SP Week 24'**.

Name	Postcode	Sales target	Sales actual
Wind	SW11 5ND	19	28
Sokoloff	SW11 5NS	32	42
Meadows	SE11 2PQ	37	38
Major	SW1 7MN	20	30
Kassam	SW9 3DZ	41	41
Smith	SW8 8LL	44	80
O'Leary	SE20 2DW	48	50

Task 4

a) In the next blank column (column D), use formulas to multiply the amount of sales made in pounds (£) by £25 per item

b) Give column D the title **'Total sales £'**.

Task 5

a) Use a formula to total columns labelled sales target, sales actual and Total sales £ columns.

b) Insert a column between columns B and C and name it Sales target £.

c) Use a formula to calculate the sales target in pounds (£)

d) Use the spell check tool to identify and correct any spelling errors in the worksheet. (Assume that employee names have been spelt correctly.)

Task 6

In the next blank column (column F)

a) Input the heading 'Difference between target and actual sales'

b) Use formulas to subtract the 'Sales actual' in column C from the 'Sales target' in column E

c) Use a formula to total the column

Task 7

In the next blank column (column G)

a) Input the heading '**weekly wage**'.

b) Use formulas to multiply the Sales actual in Column D by the rate of £5.

c) Use a formula to total the column.

Task 8

When Simply Pretty weekly sales reach a certain amount, the management awards their staff a bonus of 25% of their weekly wages.

a) In the next blank column (column H) enter the heading '**Bonus payable**'.

b) Use formulas to multiply the weekly wage figures in column G and multiply by 25% to calculate the bonus payable in column H.

c) Total the Bonus Payable column using a formula.

Task 9

Ensure that the cells containing text are left aligned and cells containing figures are right aligned.

Task 10

Ensure that all data is in Arial font, size 12. Format all figures in columns Weekly Wage and Bonus Payable columns (columns G and H) to show pounds (£) to two decimal places

Task 11

Make changes to the worksheet as follows:

a) Format the text of all column headings with a blue font colour, italics, underlining and a font size of 14.

b) Ensure that all figures and headings are visible by adjusting column widths and heights as necessary. Use wrap text where appropriate.

Task 12

a) Apply a yellow fill and double underlining to all column total cells.

b) Format all data within the column total cells with bold and italics.

Task 13

a) Insert a row above all of the data

b) Enter the heading 'Simply Pretty Week 24 Sales Staff Wages' into cell A1

c) Change the font type to Verdana and font size 16

d) Format the heading text to be in italics and underlined

Task 14

a) Ensure that the footer contains the following information: 'your name, AAT number and the date'

b) Add a time stamp to the worksheet within the footer and make sure it is readable

c) Print this worksheet ensuring that the page orientation is landscape and that all data fit onto one page by altering margins or by scaling to fit. Make sure the whole worksheet is readable and ensure that the content of every cell is visible.

Task 15

Your manager has asked you to produce a column chart showing the amount of bonuses to be paid out in week 24 for each member of staff by name.

Create the column chart and ensure that you do the following:

a) Add data labels

b) Add the chart title '**Simply Pretty Week 24 Sales Staff Bonuses**'

c) Add axis labels

d) Move the chart below the data, so that the top border of the chart area sits on row 13

e) Resize the chart so that the chart area stretches from column A to column H

f) Use a blue pattern to fill the data series (Choose any pattern style you wish)

Task 16

a) Create a footer on your chart containing the following information: '**your name, AAT number and the date**'

b) Print only the chart using portrait page orientation, ensuring it fits on one page by making adjustments to the margin size if appropriate.

KAPLAN PUBLISHING

Mock Assessment Answers

The answers to the Mock Assessments featured in this Study Text have not been included to enable more testing assessment-style conditions for students.

To access the answers, please either ask your tutor or contact Kaplan Publishing using the following e-mail address: publishing@kaplan.co.uk

INDEX

KAPLAN PUBLISHING